D0554278

ANCIENT AND MODERN IMAGES OF SAPPHO

Translations and Studies in Archaic Greek Love Lyric

Jeffrey M. Duban

UNIVERSITY
PRESS OF
AMERICA

NOV 0 1 1985

LANHAM • NEW YORK • LONDON

Copyright © 1983 by

University Press of America,™ Inc.

4720 Boston Way
Lanham, MD 20706

3 Henrietta Street
London WC2E 8LU England

Printed in the United States of America

ISBN (Perfect): 0-8191-3561-5
ISBN (Cloth): 0-8191-3560-7

Co-published by arrangement with the Classical Association of the Atlantic States

All University Press of America books are produced on acid-free
paper which exceeds the minimum standards set by the National
Historical Publications and Records Commission.

In memory of my father

Edmund I. Duban, 1908-1956
Doctorat d'Etat, Sorbonne, 1952

and

for my mother

Sylvia Mould Duban
a woman of valor

Acknowledgments

I would like to record my thanks and appreciation to those whose encouragement and assistance have contributed to the completion of this work -- to Rebekah Rice and Sarah Gratz for their confidence during the earlier phases of this work, and, from the earliest phase, to Judith Hallett, *namque tu solebas* . . ., to colleague Janice Benario for unstinting support in this, as in every, endeavor, to Herbert Benario for urging and supporting the work's publication at the University Press of America, to Charles Babcock and Mark Morford whose ever solicitous concern has, *multa inter alia*, often focused on my translation efforts, to Richard LaFleur, for encouraging the practice of translation and making me a part of the enterprise, to Taffy Stills and Carolyn Alexander, respectively, for expert typing and editing of the finished text. Particular thanks are due Mary Lefkowitz and Harry Rutledge whose reflective critiques have assured the greater accuracy and worthiness this volume would otherwise have lacked.

TABLE OF CONTENTS

Abbreviations*

BICS   *Bulletin, Institute of Classical Studies of the University of London*

CJ   *Classical Journal*

CP   *Classical Philology*

CW   *Classical World*

GRBS   *Greek, Roman and Byzantine Studies*

JHS   *Journal of Hellenic Studies*

TAPA   *Transactions of the American Philological Association*

YCS   *Yale Classical Studies*

Il.   Homer's *Iliad*
Od.   Homer's *Odyssey*
Th.   Hesiod's *Theogony*
WD   Hesiod's *Works and Days*

Frag. Adesp.: a fragment of unknown authorship (Gr., *adespoton* "without a master")

lit.   literally
Gr.   Greek
ad. loc. ad locum "at the place," where, as with a line by line commentary, a citation may be found without page number.

*Works cited three times or more are noted by author's name and page number. Full reference appears in the bibliography. Other works are generally cited in full, *ad. loc.*, and tend to be of a more specialized nature. For § 75 I have provided a separate bibliography.

x

Rhyme is the native condition of lyric verse in English; a rhymeless lyric is a maimed thing, and halts and stammers in the delivery of its message. . . . To throw away the natural grace of rhyme from a modern song is a wilful abdication of half the charm of the verse.

A. C. Swinburne, 1869

In English the condition for doing without rhyme is that the meter must be uniform and clear; . . . Of course, there is a strong spirit abroad which tries to throw off rules and exactitude. It is proud of trusting not to measured feet, but merely to its ear, . . . Unfortunately, it hates a correct ear almost as much as a measured foot.

G. Murray, 1927

Reductionist, minimalist poetics has held sway now for approximately one generation. "Open forms," if we are to believe Denise Levertov, indicate an "open mind"; "closed forms," its opposite. When in doubt drop rhyme, meter, rhythm, diction. What is important is not doing what is difficult, what takes training and much hard work, but expressing yourself.

E. George, 1982

I

PREFACE

The present work differs from most translations of Greek lyric currently available. That the translator knows Greek is the least of such differences.[1] The

[1]Roche (p. xviii) speaks of himself as exercising restraint (in translating the texts, and not his "own Sappho") at a time when imitations have once again become fashionable: "Poets up and down the land are writing their own Homers and Ovids and Virgils: *some of them without reference to or even knowledge of the language from which they quarry their ore of gold*" (emphasis added). That the "best of them follow an old and lively tradition" is of no consolation. The "tradition" thrives in recent years among translators who "get along with a little help from their friends." Admissions of inadequacy in the understanding of Greek have been either veiled or ingenuously avowed. Thus Davenport (pp. 14-16): "My starting point was the poems and not the Greek language, my knowledge of which is functional rather than philological [?] . . . . The reading of Sappho is surrounded by passionate dispute in which I am unqualified to join; my translation therefore is without authority except the dubious one of sentiment . . . . To approach the emotions of ancient poets is a matter helped along by more than halting Greek, dictionaries, and history books; my debt therefore extends to . . . ." So also Ayrton (p. 3): "I do not know much Greek and so Geoffrey Kirk has made me a literal translation of the existing texts, all that can be comprehensibly transcribed of them. I took this and I acknowledge also a debt to Richard [*sic*] Lattimore, Guy Davenport [!], F. Lasserre, D. A. Campbell and others, whose translations and discourses I have read. But I rashly composed this text myself" [!]. Barnstone's 610 selection rendering of lyric authors from the 8th century B.C. to the 6th A.D. (still the most comprehensive undertaking of its kind) can only inspire amazement as the product of a comparatist whose primary training is in Spanish. Such temerity is not confined to the slender lyricists. Even Homer can no longer find a poet-scholar-translator. See Denison Hall tr., *The Odyssey* (Greenwich 1978), p. xi: "So, knowing little English [sc. poetry] and less Greek, I decided to do it [i.e. translate Homer] myself."
For the practice of team translation ("as much flawed ethically as it is aesthetically"), see E. George, "Translating Poetry: Notes on a Solitary Craft," *Kenyon Review*, Vol. 4 (1982), pp. 33-54; also, C. R. Beye, "Reupholstering Greek Tragedy," *Parnassus*, Vol. 6 (1977), pp. 289-304.

volume is, first, a collection of love lyrics alone.
Until now, such lyrics have appeared in anthologies of
Greek lyric poems of all kinds: eulogies, political
odes, victory odes, etc.[2] Because of Sappho's high
standing and particular appeal, and the number of
fragments in which she survives, she, more often than
the others in this translation, has merited treatment
in a separate volume and in her entirety. This has re-
sulted in the often pretentious appearance of page af-
ter page with no more than one to three words each.[3]
Moreover, the translator of Greek lyric poetry, when
not dutifully bracketing *lacunae* ("bracketology")[4] or
zealously enshrining isolated words and phrases, can
as readily be found converting fancy to context[5] or
improving upon such context as already exists.[6] It is,

---

[2]For the forms and origins of Greek lyric see Bowra, pp. 1-
15, and W. McCulloh's introduction to Barnstone, pp. 2-13.
    [3]So Grodon. Roche, however, puts several such one to three
word combinations to the page.
    [4]My use of brackets is limited. In most cases I offer a
consecutive rendering while noting the fragmentary nature of the
text. Words within brackets are based on conjecture.
    [5]Such invention usually follows the ingenious but perverse
"reconstructions" of J. M. Edmonds (see bibliography), e.g.,
Roche (p. 164): "The Greek text I have used is based on that
edition by J. M. Edmonds . . . , with emendations from Page,
Haines, Hill, and others (and in a few instances my own)." We
are, then, not surprised to find more of Sappho "surviving" in
Roche's than in any other contemporary translation.
    [6]So Davenport (p. 95) -- to take one of many examples --
renders my *§* 36: "Percussion, salt and honey,/A quivering in the
thighs:/He shakes me all over again,/Eros who cannot be thrown,/
Who stalks on all fours/Like a beast." Beyond the unacknowledged
source in H.D. of the phrase "salt and honey," this is one of
two renderings that Davenport, as elsewhere, offers: "Several
times I have given alternate translations . . . since no English
version of language so remote in idiom and estranged in culture
can be in any sense wholly accurate or final" (p. 14). This,
from the translator whose intention, two sentences later,
"everywhere has been to suggest the tone of Sappho's words."
Proverb has it that he with no excuse gives two.

2

then, context, no less than content, which has deter-
mined the selections for this volume: only such love
lyrics as have or suggest a context (or *sense*) have
found inclusion.

More significant is my pervasive use of rhyme and
meter. Though at another time this was much the prac-
tice, no contemporary, or "modern," translation of
Greek lyric has made the attempt. Rhyme and meter, we
are to understand, are somehow uncontemporary, passé.
Thus, to their many liberties of content, translators
as often bring an unruliness of form, and an idiom,
mundane or grandiose, in turn. The result wins ready
approval from the present generation (the ironest of
all), nurtured on the wayward progeny of Walt Whitman,
captivated by the writings of e. e. cummings, and
indoctrinated with such heady notions as the demo-
cratization of poetry and Everyman as poet, be it
standard bearer of the recondite or chronicler of the
commonplace. The poet Horace's words ring as true
today as they did in Rome of the 1st century, B.C.:
scribimus indocti doctique poemata passim: "Everybody
and his uncle thinks he's a poet."[7]

The same lack of discrimination and proportion is
apparent in the other arts. The concrete poem (within
its "play-area") is in good company with the paint
blotch on the canvas, the chaos of mass and matter in
sculpture, the plague of cacophony at Symphony Hall.[8]

---

[7]Horace, *Epistles* 2.1.117, lit., "We write poems indiscrim-
inately, the learned and unlearned, alike."

[8]One can usually tell when a conductor "addresses the audi-
ence" that it is going to be "one of those pieces."

Will the need for more room eventually move ballet outdoors?[9]

"Until very recently," observes Willis Barnstone in his introduction (p. 18), "it has been a uniform practice to *impose* [italics supplied] rhyme on poems from ancient Greek. But the Greeks did not use end rhyme as a common poetic device . . ., and so rhyme is not used in these translations."[10] It is only in the added labor and stricter discipline which rhyme requires that the use of rhyme becomes an *imposition*. So also the use of meter. It is, moreover, precisely the absence from Greek poetry of rhyme and meter *as we know it* that is responsible for the pervasive freedom

[9]Those who prefer order over chaos will find welcome confirmation of their preference in Eugenio Montale's brief essay "The Second Life of Art," in the *New York Review of Books*, April 16, 1981, pp. 19-20 (first published in 1949!): ". . . [A] coarse materialization of the artistic act is at the root of many of today's experiments. . . . A musical arabesque which is not a 'motif' or idea because the ear does not perceive it as such, a theme which is not a theme because it will never be recognizable, a line or group of lines . . . which can never come back to us . . . , do not truly belong to the world of form, of expressed art." In a similar vein, see J. D. Reed, "Synthesizer Chic in North Carolina: But whatever happened to intimacy and grace?" in *Time*, July 27, 1981, pp. 42-43. As in the piece by Montale, the issue is one of communicability.

[10]I know of no such "very recent" practice. Groden (p. xxii) makes a similar *apologia* for meter: "The poems of this translation will be found to lack formal meter. Greek meter is based primarily on quantity, . . . English meter . . . on stress . . . . English poetry has no exact equivalent of the Greek concept, and no attempt has been made to make do with an inexact one." Groden proceeds to add her own objective to the impossibilities of their kind (discussed below, p. 9). "It seemed preferable to set out the words, ideas, and images of the original [= the original poem, I take it] as clearly as possible in their translated form, arranging them in such a way that they might create visually some of the effects of stress and relationship that were achieved by sound and word order in the Greek." Groden does not, however, disappoint in her hope "that the language of the English translation is not totally lacking in rhythm and balance."

4

of form and content in translation today. This freedom tends ever to distance the translation from its original meaning and intensity. Despite frequent avowals to the contrary, there is no way that the essential features of Greek poetry -- a quantitative (as opposed to accentual) meter, a highly inflected, polysyllabic, vowel-rich vocabulary, a broadly flexible word-order -- can be rendered into English or any language.

A comparison of first stanza renderings of Sappho's great *Hymn to Aphrodite* will illustrate the bewildering variety of form and content that the Greekless reader encounters if reading more than a single version. Before comparing and commenting on such versions I will transliterate that stanza, provide a literal translation,[11] and explain the principle of its original rhythm.

> — u — u — u u — u — u
> Poikilóthron' athanát' Aphródita,
>
> — u— u — u u — u — u
> paî Díos, dolóploke, líssomaí se,
>
> — u —. u — u u— u — —
> mé m'ássaisi méd' oníaisi dámna
>
> — u u — u
> pótnia thûmon.

> Flower-appareled,[12] deathless Aphrodite,
> child of Zeus, weaver of wiles, I beg you,
> do not subdue me [*me m'. . .damna*] with
> distress or anguish, lady, (in my) heart.

[11] I would note that C. M. Bowra's literal renderings are in the majority of cases superior to what has passed in recent years for literary translation. Bowra's poetic prose reflects the sensibility of an age when rhymed and metered translation was the norm.

[12] See § 1.1, note.

The rhythm of a Sapphic stanza (§§ 1-4) consists of a thrice repeated —ᴗ — $\underline{\text{ᴗ}}$ —ᴗᴗ —ᴗ — $\underline{\text{ᴗ}}$ followed by the Epic "tag" —ᴗᴗ — $\underline{\text{ᴗ}}$ [13] (i.e., the line-ending cadence of all Epic poetry -- Homer, Hesiod, Virgil, etc.[14]). As noted above, this, as all classical poetry, is quantitative in nature: it is the long or short quantity of each vowel that determines the length -- long (two beats) or short (one beat) -- of the syllable in which it appears.[15] The accent marks appearing between the metric "long" or "short" and the letter itself indicate the words' *spoken* stress, that is,

---

[13] $\underline{\text{ᴗ}}$ indicates the syllable may be either long or short. A syllable is long if it contains a naturally long vowel or a short vowel followed by two consonants in the same or in consecutive words (= long "by position").

[14] The meter of Epic poetry is dactylic hexameter:

$$\_\,\overline{\text{ᴗᴗ}} \; \_\,\overline{\text{ᴗᴗ}} \; \_\,\overline{\text{ᴗᴗ}} \; \_\,\overline{\text{ᴗᴗ}} \; \_\,\text{ᴗᴗ} \; \_\,\underline{\text{ᴗ}}$$

. It is the most abundantly preserved of all classical meters and was often used in the composition of non-Epic works, Greek and Latin: bucolics, satire, epistles (sometimes dealing with literary criticism), and others. Longfellow's *Evangeline* is perhaps the most familiar example of the hexameter's adaptation into English.

[15] The following is a simplification for the general reader. Greek verse did not, in point of fact, significantly operate with a stress accent, nor was it measured by a regular musical "beat." In other words, the quantitative "longum" does not technically constitute a stressed syllable, as the alternation of such syllables does not technically produce "rhythm." See W. B. Stanford, *The Sound of Greek* (Berkeley: U. of California Press 1967), pp. 40-43, 157-160, and the pioneering work by P. Maas, *Greek Metre*, H. Lloyd-Jones trans. (Oxford: Clarendon Press 1962), p. 3-4 (first published as *Griechische Metrik*, 1923). Pitch, not stress, seems to have been the determining factor (see Stanford, *ibid*). Even so, for the purposes of this discussion, I follow the practice adopted by G. Thomson, *Greek Lyric Meter* (Cambridge: Cambridge U. Press 1929), p. 7, n. 2, of "marking the rhythmical beat on those syllables [i.e., the 'longa'] where, to an English ear, it would naturally fall." Notes Thomson (*ibid.*): "Whether the Greeks recognised a rhythmical beat, or *ictus*, is not certain . . . : but the modern reader will find it easier to distinguish between the various Greek rhythms if he assumes that they did."

where the word would be accented if it appeared, let us assume, in a prose line. In a system of this kind, the poetic stress (i.e., any "long") is in many cases superimposed upon (and runs counter to) a word's spoken stress, or accent (e.g., $a\overset{\prime}{t}ha\overset{\cup}{n}\overset{\cup}{a}t'$). Theoretically, then, two rhythms are simultaneously operative.[16] Where poetic stress falls on an unaccented syllable, the word assumes an alternative (e.g., $D\overset{\cup}{i}\overset{\prime}{o}s$) or even a second (e.g., $po\overset{\prime}{i}k\overset{\cup}{i}l\overset{—}{o}\,thr\overset{\cup}{o}n'$) stress. The desired end of this "superimposition" is the avoidance of complete, or even too frequent, coincidence between word-ending and poetic foot-ending (e.g., $pa\overset{—}{t}\,D\overset{\cup}{i}o\,\overset{—}{s}$ $\overset{\cup}{d}o\overset{—}{l}\overset{\cup}{o}\,pl\overset{\cup}{o}ke$). Were the coincidence excessive (e.g., a continuation of the first verse's pattern) the effect would be prosaic. The same effect would result from a frequent correspondence between poetic and spoken stress.

That this is what occurs in English *accentual* verse does not render the result prosaic. The alternation of stressed and unstressed syllables has nothing

---

[16]I cannot agree with Roche's (pp. 149-152) "Greek Meters: Outline to a New Approach": ". . . the two schemes of metric, quantity and stress, do *not* in fact run counter to each other, but parallel, and possess between them a perfect analogy of metric. What has been left out is this: the fact that Greek and English share (on top of their metrical heritages) a treasury of spoken rhythms where quantity and stress become almost interchangeable terms." Roche's thesis suffers from his exclusive reliance on monosyllables to illustrate English words with variable stress. The one polysyllable, "*Hickery*," of mouse and clock fame, would easily lend itself to manipulation as a nonsense word.

to do with long or short vowel quantity.[17] An English
Sapphic "imitation" will best illustrate the point.
One could do no better than to quote from Swinburne,
for whom Sappho was "simply nothing less -- as she is
certainly nothing more -- than the greatest poet who
ever was at all":[18]

Áll the níght sléep cáme not upón my éyelids,
Shed not dew, nor shook nor unclosed a feather,
Yet with lips shut close and with eyes of iron
    Stood and beheld me.

Then to me so lying awake a vision
Came without sleep over the seas and touched me,
Softly touched my eyelids and lips; and I too,
    Full of the vision,

Saw the white implacable Aphrodite,
Saw the hair unbound and the feet unsandalled
Shine as fire of sunset on Western waters;
    Saw the reluctant

Feet, the straining plumes of the doves that drew her,
Looking always, looking with necks reverted,
Back to Lesbos, back to the hills where under
    Shone Mitylene;

Heard the flying feet of the Loves behind her
Make a sudden thunder upon the waters,
As the thunder flung from the strong unclosing
    Wings of a great wind.

[17]For attempts at quantitative meter in English, see H.
Gross, *Sound and Form in Modern Poetry* (Ann Arbor: Univ. of
Michigan Press 1964), pp. 32-38, and C. O. Hartman, *Free Verse*
(Princeton: Princeton Univ. Press 1980), pp. 33-39.
   [18]A. C. Swinburne, "Sappho," *Saturday Review* 117 (1914), Feb.
21. The full text appears in Appendix II. The following quote is
from the poet's *Sapphics* (the first five of twenty such
stanzas). See *The Works of Algernon Charles Swinburne: Poems*,
David McKay, Publisher (Philadelphia, n.d.), pp. 82-84. For
recent discussion of Sappho's influence on Swinburne, see M. B.
Raymond, *Swinburne's Poetics: Theory and Practice* (The Hague:
Mouton 1971), pp. 57-86 *passim*.

The poetic rhythm results from an ordering of words in accordance with their natural, or "spoken," stress (i.e., *eyelids* is always stressed on the first syllable): poetic and spoken stress thus coincide. Given this one of several essential differences between Greek and English verse, we must be wary of such as propose in translation to "give some idea of the variety within Sappho's verbal fabric: her flux of texture . . .: to reflect a little of her elusiveness, shift of tempos, subtleties of echo within technique or mood." Likewise the most recent, though less ambitious, intention of "suggesting the tone of Sappho's words."[19] We may now proceed with comparison of the *Hymn to Aphrodite*'s opening stanza.

Davenport:
God's stunning daughter deathless Aphródita,
A whittled perplexity your bright abstruse chair,
Don't blunt my stubborn eye with breathlessness, lady,
To tame my heart.

The points to be made are many:[20] the use of "God" for "Zeus" shows no sign of abating as a persistent flaw

[19]Quotes are from Roche, p. xx, and Davenport, p. 14, respectively. See also note 10, above. It is beyond my ability to determine just what Roche intends by "subtleties of echo within technique or mood" or how such subtleties might be conveyed: an example of "translationese."

[20]I note C. R. Beye's highly favorable review of the Davenport translation ("Greek Lyrics in and out of Brackets," *Parnassus*, Vol. 9 [1981] pp. 200–216), and, with all due regard for my undergraduate mentor and friend, my point for point disagreement.

of translation.[21] The Judeo-Christian association will thus continue to confuse the unknowing student or general reader. "Stunning"[22] has no connection with the word it purports to translate, *doloploke* "weaver of wiles," and is by our understanding of the word today, certainly foreign to any notion in ancient Greek. The transliteration of Aphrodite's name "Aphródita" must strike the knowing reader as peculiar on two counts: it is nowhere the practice to render the Aeolic form into English,[23] while the spoken stress as indicated for the second syllable is in any case superseded by the poetic stress of the Greek.[24] The second line is an inexplicable elaboration of the poem's first word, a rhapsody on a non-existent theme, while the third line,[25] with its gratuitous introduction of an "eye"

---

[21]And of the translation of Greek tragedy in particular. What passes for "God" in translation is usually either *theos* or *daimon* in Greek, "a (the) divinity." The term may refer to a specific god (whom we know from the general context, Apollo, Dionysus, etc.) or, more broadly, to divine agency (when it can be equivalent with Zeus whose will is Fate).

[22]The word appears in place of "wildering" in Davenport's 1965 edition. This, and the change as noted in n. 25, below, are the only differences in the two versions of the poem. One wonders what has been gained.

[23]Despite Barnstone's observation (p. 18) concerning the increased tendency in recent years to use English transliteration for Greek words ("a new practice . . . with rules unfixed, used differently by different hands"), the practice does not extend to the transliteration of proper names *in dialectical variants*.

[24]Indication of spoken stress is further without point because Aeolic accentuation in all words except prepositions is recessive, i.e., appears on the third-to-last syllable unless the last syllable is long, in which case the accent moves up to the second-to-last. (Aeolic disyllables are accented on the first syllable.) Hence, *Aphrodíte* in Homer, *Aphrodítta* in Sappho; though *Aphródita* in the Greek text of *S* 1.1 because the vocative ending is short. See further J. T. Hooker, pp. 18–23.

[25]"With heartbreak, lady, and breathlessness/Tame not my heart" in the 1965 edition.

-- and its proposed "blunting" -- leaves us breathless indeed. How "taming the heart" logically follows defies explanation. A passing note on syllabification: the line lengths (11, 12, 10, 4) are matched neither in sequence nor consistency in any of the other stanzas -- indeed, no two stanzas are alike -- which range from 30-39 beats each. So much for "suggesting the tone of Sappho's words."

Barnstone:

On your dazzling throne, Aphrodite,
sly eternal daughter of Zeus,
I beg you: do not crush my heart with grief, . . ."

The first of seven such stanzas; syllabification fairly consistent. The third verse appears flatly monosyllabic and hence, prosaic. So also "sly" as a rendering for the compound *doloploke*. Moreover, "do not crush me with grief" lacks the fullness of the original's "do not subdue me with distress or anguish, lady, (in my) heart." The rendering is short on texture, and would have doubtless benefited from a +3 beat extended line and inclusion of a fourth line "tag."

Roche:

Undying Aphrodite on your caparisoned throne,
Daughter of Zeus and weaver of ruses --
    Now, I address you:

Queen, do not hurt my heart, do not harry it . . .

Roche begins the second stanza of his translation before completing the first stanza of the original. As the shortfall will have somewhere to be compensated for, we are not surprised to find a final stanza of five lines. "Address" is too neutral for the Greek

11

lissomai "implore, beseech," while "harry" seems to reflect a poorly perceived need for alliteration, as the word is little suited to matters of the heart. A similar need, this time for assonance, seems apparent in the choice of "ruses" (with "Zeus"). Better, I think, the alliteration, even if traditional, of "weaver of wiles."

Groden:

Eternal Aphrodite, rainbow-throned,
you cunning, wily child of Zeus, I beg you,
do not break me, lady,
with pains and raging ills of love.

Aside from the fanciful and potentially misleading rainbow-throned (Is Aphrodite enthroned *on* a rainbow?), the content and rhythm of these lines is appealing. Neither, however, is systematically developed or sustained as we read on in a prosy version of three "stanzas" whose 18, 8 and 3 verses vary anywhere from 2 to 13 beats each (see n. 10, above).

Barnard:

Dapple-throned Aphrodite,
eternal daughter of God,
snare-knitter! Don't, I beg you,

cow my heart with grief! . . ."

The first 3 lines are the first of ten such stanzas. The rendering, on the whole, is the most rhythmically appealing of the several cited. Still, "Zeus" would have served as a perfectly suitable alternative to "God," while a more energetic diction would have alleviated the monosyllabic run: "Don't, I beg you,/cow my heart with grief!" "Cow," moreover, does not reflect an appealing sense of *mot juste* (surely "crush" might have done), while "snare-knitter" is not given to particularly facile pronunciation.

Lattimore:

Throned in splendor, deathless, O Aphrodite,
child of Zeus, charm fashioner, I entreat you
not with grief and bitternesses to break my
spirit, O goddess . . .

Lattimore, here as throughout the four significant pieces in Sapphic stanza, precisely reproduces the syllabification, and to large extent, rhythm of the original (though "bitternesses" is heavy going). The opening stanza is appealing, and the poem overall, attractive. Inasmuch as Lattimore's is a superior rendering,[26] it is regrettable that he chose to keep his work within the strictest confines of a "selection." He translates only nine pieces by Sappho and only slightly more than one quarter of the selections contained in this volume.

Duban:

Appareled in flowered allure, deathless,
deceiver, daughter of Zeus, Aphrodite,
subdue not, nor destroy, this heart, my lady,
with distress, . . .

My own version, as exemplified by the first stanza, adheres to a long line of either 10 or 11 beats, and a "tag" of 3 or, in the last two stanzas, 4. Next to

---

[26]Superior in sensibility, though not always in sense. Notes R. J. Tarrant (p. 7): "His handling of lyric is less even [than his treatment of early elegy]. Sappho in particular suffers from inaccuracy, excessive restoration, and clumsy phrasing" (examples, p. 8).

Lattimore's it is the most consistent in this respect, and closest to the original.[27] But what it may lose in exact correspondence to the original, it gains in the sense of articulation, from stanza to stanza, produced by rhyme. The rhyme equivalent $-\,\overset{\cup\cup}{}\,-\,-$ of the original would impart a similar sense of stanza.

Had I not decided on a rhymed approximation of the Sapphic stanza, I would have attempted to bring a similar consistency to whatever form and/or rhyme scheme I had chosen. Such is my practice in the longer "non-Sapphic" structures, as in the shorter pieces, throughout.[28] The rhyme schemes and metric of this volume are, then, all of my own making. Such means are thoroughly "traditional," even if their application to Greek lyric poetry in the last fifty years is not. I have, moreover, attempted to maintain a sense of fluid and varied rhythm by avoidance of uneventful monosyllabic runs and by the frequent use of enjambment.

A brief comparison with Lattimore's rendering of § 2 will show, beyond such incidence as already noted in Barnstone and Barnard, what monosyllabic tendencies seem best avoided.

Like the very gods in my sight *is he who*
sits where he can look in your eyes, who listens
close to you, to hear the soft voice, its sweetness
      murmur in love and

[27]In my remaining Sapphics (§§ 2-4), the long lines range from 7 to 10, the "tag," from 3-5 beats, each. Even so, no single stanza (except when fragmentary) varies overall by more than 3 beats from a stanza within the same poem.

[28]Again, with the exception of various fragmentary contexts, e.g., §§ 4.14-16, 40.67-75; but compare § 3.8-11.

14

laughter, all for him. But it breaks my spirit;
underneath my breast all the heart is shaken.
Let me only glance where you are, the voice dies,
       I can say nothing,

but my lips are stricken to silence, under-
neath my skin the tenuous flame suffuses;
nothing shows in front of my eyes, my ears are
       muted in thunder.

And the sweat breaks running upon me, fever
shakes my body, paler I turn than grass is;
I can feel that I have been changed, *I feel that*
       death *has* come near me.

First, the italicized words of the opening and closing verses, viz., the repeated pronouns and cumbersome auxiliaries, do little to move the thought dramatically along. Though monosyllabic runs may indeed be eventful in their own right, the likelihood lessens with the increase of prepositions, articles, pronouns, and sometimes conjunctions: the "little words," like so much flotsam, accumulate to impede the flow, or, as in the present case, to fill the line. Lattimore uses "the" six times to my three, "in" five times to my zero, and "my" eight times to my six -- an overall instance of more than two to one. In the last stanza alone, Lattimore uses seven pronouns to my four (the Greek has two as direct and indirect object, and two contained in first person verb forms). Moreover, his three "can" + verb constructions (all monosyllabic) and four passives, all requiring auxiliaries (there are no passives in the Greek), likewise attenuate the momentum.

    The Greek, we may note, abounds in conjunctions, many of them monosyllabic. Each verse from line 7 onward contains at least one. Charles Segal (p. 147) notes "The polysyndeton [which] enhances the effect of accumulating intensity [and] also creates a rhythmical tempo of excitement and mounting tension analogous to the ritualizing effects of dance or drum beat." Inasmuch as conjunctions are joining words, they tend, by their nature, to move the thought along, not to impede it. Moreover, even when they accumulate as rapidly as in § 2, they tend still not to clutter: four of seven uses of *de* "and" (lines 10-15) are elided to *d'* when the word following begins with a vowel. The elided forms, pronounced as part of the word following, are syllabically negligible.

I have sought as well to avoid commonplaces of diction and sentiment (often the accompaniment of excessive monosyllabics). Yet within such constraints, I have been as playful as assonance and alliteration might allow. Such devising is well suited to a central theme in many of the poems (Anacreon's and Archilochus' especially), that of "play" itself (Gr., *paizein* "to play," always with an erotic connotation). To the extent that such devices succeed, they will go unnoted.

As I have attempted before all else to make a poem in English, it is hoped the poetry of my translation commends itself as such to readers of English as did the original to readers (or listeners) of Greek. Such equivalence is possible only through means that succeed in their own right,[29] and not through some benighted hope of suggesting Sappho's tone, verbal fabric, flux of texture, and the like. I will be

[29]Though Barnstone makes precisely this point, I cannot say it is validated by the end product of his translation: "A poem in translation should be faithful, if to anything, to [the] primary quality of the original -- that of its being an effective poem" (p. 19) . . . . "The quality of the poem in translation will depend on the translator's skill in writing poetry in his own language in the act of translating" (p. 20).

fabric, flux of texture, and the like. I will be pleased in those readers who have in the pages of this translation found refuge from the plague of modernity. Readers who find the translation uncontemporary or "archaic"[30] -- and who disallow the possibility of studying Greek -- will perhaps find what they require in my predecessors' work.

It is often said of poetic translation that it is incapable of being both beautiful and faithful at once. The present response stems largely from my feeling that most translations of ancient Greek lyric have, at their best, been faithful alone. In attempting to combine both qualities, I may at times have sacrificed the more mundane of the two. If so, I have always preferred FitzGerald's flask of wine and book of verse to the mancel loaf and mutton haunch of Robert Graves.

J. M. D.

Boston, Mansfield and Atlanta,
1975-1983

---

[30]If "middle main" (*§* 1.12) or "neath" (*§* 2.10) together with other such usages appear "archaic," I can only hope that such "lapses" seem negligible in the end result.

II

INTRODUCTION

As the aim of the introduction and end-notes
has been not so much originality as synthe-
sis, the two sections freely draw from
ancient testimonia (for basically factual
materials)[31] and from contemporary writings
(for broadly interpretive materials). Hence,
the frequency of paraphrase and/or quotation
in hopes of having condensed the best of the
best. I have, as well, intentionally de-
emphasized strictly biographical informa-
tion. That Archilochus lived from 680 - 640
and was the son of a Parian aristocrat and a
slave woman, that Alcman is sometimes
thought to have been a Lydian from Sardis,
sometimes a Laconian from Messoa is informa-
tion as often recorded as it is quickly for-
gotten. On the reliability and use of bio-
graphical notices see now M. Lefkowitz, *The
Lives of the Greek Poets*, Baltimore: Johns
Hopkins Univ. Press, 1982.

PROSPECTUS

The lyrics of this volume were composed in the
7th and 6th centuries B.C. on both sides of the Aegean
and in between: Alcman of Sparta in the Peloponnese;
Anacreon of Teos on the Greek populated coast of
Ionia, or Asia Minor (modern Turkey); and Sappho,
Archilochus and Ibycus on the islands of Lesbos, Paros

[31]Ancient testimonia for Sappho appear, with facing English
translation, in Campbell 1982.

and Samos.[32] Archilochus and Ibycus composed basically in the Ionic, or Epic, dialect of Homer and Hesiod; Anacreon, in a literary Ionic with relatively few epicisms; Alcman, in a Spartan, or Doric, dialect; and Sappho, in what is for the modern reader of ancient Greek, the most difficult of all Greek dialects: Aeolic.[33] The poets were steeped in the Homeric and Hesi-

[32]The Alexandrians reckoned a canon of nine lyric poets' which, while excluding Archilochus on formal grounds, also included Alcaeus (Sappho's contemporary and countryman; poetry highly political), Steisichorus (see n. 48, below), Simonides (best known today for his epitaphs of the Persian War and dirge for the heroes of Thermopylae), Pindar and Bacchylides (contemporary rival composers of the "Victory Odes" by which they are both best known today; Bacchylides the nephew of Simonides). With the last two, we come to the mid 5th century B.C. Notes Kirkwood (p. 3): "In general, the Alexandrian lists [Nine Lyric Poets, Ten Orators, Seven Tragic Poets, etc.] were selections, consisting of the writers of the highest distinction in their fields, who were to be taken as standards of excellence and as authorities for matters of style and linguistic purity." The *Palatine Anthology* preserves what may have been "mottos" for books of selections from the Nine Lyric Poets:

PINDAR of Thebes clanged a sonorous note; the Muse of SIMONIDES breathed a joy of delicious-noted sound; STEISICHORUS and IBYCUS rang clear; ALCMAN was sweet; and the lips of BACCHYLIDES uttered delights; Persuasion attended ANACREON; and Lesbian ALCAEUS spoke flowered notes to the wise Aeolian maiden [i.e., Sappho]. But SAPPHO was not ninth among the men; rather is she written tenth in the list of lovely Muses.

PINDAR, the holy mouth of the Muses; that sweetly prattling Siren, BACCHYLIDES; those Aeolian Graces of SAPPHO; the book ANACREON composed; STEISICHORUS, who drew in his own works from the stream of Homer; the sweet scroll of SIMONIDES; IBYCUS, gatherer of Persuasion's and young lads' bloom; the sword ALCAEUS used to shed the blood of tyrants and save his country's rights; the maiden-tuned nightingales of ALCMAN -- I pray you all be gracious unto me, you have established the beginning and end of all lyric song.

[33]"There is so little of Sappho," notes Davenport complacently, "that the reader with beginner's Greek can read the substantial fragments in an afternoon."

odic Epic traditions which had attained to Pan-Hellenic popularity.[34]

But unlike their Epic predecessors, the Lyric poets celebrated the great deeds of the past, not for their own sake, but because they illustrated and exalted the present. The Lyric present brims with a subjectivity unknown, or only vaguely expressed, in Epic. Personal taste over which, as the Latin proverb has it, there can be no dispute; unabashed individualism; Love as an agonizing sensation akin in its extremities to death (and not simply a power, or one of the great delights, in the cosmos); righteous indignation fueled by a growing awareness of the rift between what is and what ought to be; the ebb and flow (periodicity, cycles of change) that marks human circumstance; and, as situation and personality dictate, easy pleasantry and disconcern -- these are the hallmarks of Lyric, and of love Lyric, in particular.[35]

This poetry, and that of the period in general, survives in no regular manuscript tradition. It has reached us primarily on tattered papyri (dating from the 3rd century B.C. to the 10th A.D.) discovered, for the most part, in Egypt,[36] and in the largely partial quotations of later writers -- grammarians, metricians, lexicographers (5th century B.C. to the 12th

[34]That is, to a general acceptance throughout all Greece, an acceptance which superseded, without invalidating, the local, or "epichoric," traditions of individual regions.
[35]The foregoing paragraph is largely indebted to Snell's chapter, "The Rise of the Individual in Early Greek Lyric," pp. 43-70; highly recommended (together with Fränkel) as introductory reading.
[36]Mostly at Oxyrhynchus (modern Behnesa), situated on the edge of the western desert 120 miles south of Cairo. For the fascinating account of these discoveries by B. P. Grenfeld and A. S. Hunt at the end of the nineteenth century, see E. G. Turner, esp. pp. 27ff.

A.D.) -- who were more often motivated by the technical concerns of meter and dialect than by any appreciation of form, content, or sentiment. It is, nonetheless, to these "Dryasdusts" that we owe the preservation of much of archaic Greek love lyric.[37] Sappho's case is particularly noteworthy: she survived by way of citation and scattered papyrus because such unlikely havens of her poetry escaped the purges to which the manuscripts of her work were subjected from the first to the fifteenth century. These excesses included public burning at the hands of an over-zealous and puritanical Christianity.[38]

THE POETS IN ANTIQUITY
Archilochus

Archilochus may be considered the earliest Greek lyric poet. Though much of his vocabulary and phraseology derive from the Homeric tradition, the poet's ideas often stand at a variance with the conventional outlook found in the *Iliad* or *Odyssey* (e.g., §§ 82, 83). Archilochus, as Gerber observes (p. 9), is not a philosopher poet in search of immutable truth. "Rather he is concerned with understanding the pattern of life [esp. § 81] and, by his own intellect, with learning how to accommodate himself to the laws which govern this pattern."

---

[37]"Thanks be to the host . . . of Dryasdusts," notes Symonds (p. 275), "from whose heaps of shot rubbish Bergk and his predecessors have sorted out these fragments of extinguished stars." For the pioneering work of Bergk, see Appendix I (p. 163). Only several pieces in this collection are thought to be complete. Among them §§ 1, 38, 49, 79, 81, 91, 94. For the treatment of textual "gaps," or *lacunae*, see note 4, above.
[38]See Friedrich, pp. 126-127, for details.

The range of Archilochus' emotion is broader than that of the other poets in this volume. Such poems as §§ 78-80 reflect the heartfelt emotion of the soldier-poet and are, no less than his strictly erotic verses, poems of the heart. As such, they find their place in this collection. Archilochus is also more explicitly sexual than the others (e.g., §§ 84-88). For all its constraint and veiled allusion, § 75 is without parallel. Two of his coarser pieces I have omitted entirely -- not from any false modesty or prudishness, but because of the tone they would inject among pieces so much unlike themselves.[39]

An event of central importance to the poet, and one reflected in his work no less than in citation by later writers, was his betrothal to one Neoboule (§§ 74, 75.21) and subsequent dispossession by her father, Lycambes, who married her off to a wealthier suitor. This event is considered responsible for the particular vehemence which is the hallmark of much Archilochean poetry. The legend developed long after the poet's time that he so railed against Lycambes and his daughters that they hung themselves in desperation.

Such biographical extrapolations have, however, been recently questioned. Gregory Nagy (see § 75, bibliography) notes that "the direct textual evidence about Lykambes [or his daughters] is so deficient that we have the greatest difficulties in reconstructing the overall structure of any Archilochean composition from any of the attested fragments or excerpts." Reversing the notion that Archilochus is the *persona* whose actions determined the narrative of § 75, Nagy

---

[39]The two pieces are translated and discussed by Rankin, pp. 61-64.

argues that the invective function of the composition determined the narrative which in turn determined the *persona* that acts and speaks within. By *persona* we are to understand, in this context, "the role which is traditional for a poet to assume in a specific genre." A piece like § 75 confirms what we can also infer from other fragments, namely, an inherited custom of invective poetry with stylized characters and themes of universal no less than particular significance.[40] Such invective with its praise counterpart found social expression through the prime medium of verse.

Recent discussion of Sappho has also focussed on the public, rather than private, *persona*, on the social context and function of the poetry. I defer such discussion to "Sappho in recent criticism" (below). For the meantime, we may note a range of insightful comparisons (however autobiographically based) between her and Archilochus, as drawn by Robert Bagg (pp. 44-46): "While Archilochus shared his opinions with his fellows, Sappho shared the most elusive emotions, and to do so led her to use language far more allusively and symbolically." Archilochus is more sensually and autobiographically self-centered. However novel this perspective, it can not compare with Sappho's "sudden divination of her own personality's ability to comfort and anchor others." Archilochus' "first remarkable intuition of self" is ultimately self-limiting: "His relentless squaring-off against other people perhaps prevents an understanding of his friends' effects on him or what he gives to them. It is the whole give and take of his sympathy, the emotional interdependence of

---

[40]The approach is anticipated by K. J. Dover (1964), pp. 212-216, who speaks of the "assumed personality and the imaginary situation."

people, which is missing from Archilochus' glimpse of the self . . . . [Sappho's voice by contrast] seems so vulnerable and introspective, though it is if anything more confirmed in its pride. The audience suddenly shrinks from an entire city to a few close friends, and in this new situation, the autobiographical poet finds that her own voice may assume and register their personal problems and qualities . . . . Archilochus' work is tense with feeling, but we never forget that it is his feeling before it is ours. He presents himself as pleasured or ravaged by an event, alone, with no company . . . . Archilochus' genius was to use autobiography to make himself as distinct as possible from everybody else."[41]

Alcman

Alcman is the earliest choral composer whose work survives in substantial fragments. The grace and gaiety of the scenes Alcman portrays are in accord with what archaeology and literary reference indicate about Sparta in the 7th and 6th centuries: "Youth's mettle and the clear-tuned Muse bloom there."[42] It was only later, after the 5th century, that Sparta became the type of city which has left its namesake in our vocabulary.

Where Archilochus addresses his fellow citizens, Alcman composes, more than any other, for his own city, and in such a way as to give his work, in Campbell's words (p. 194), a "strong, provincial, almost parochial," flavor. He was fond too of reference

---

[41]Such contrast must call into question the notion (Bowra, p. 240; Gerber, p. 161) of Sappho as "a feminine counterpart of Archilochus."

[42]The phrase is ascribed to the mid 7th century musician and poet, Terpander of Lesbos, whose works survive in dubiously authentic fragments.

to obscure foreign tribes, real and fabulous, to the perplexity of scholars both ancient and modern.[43]

Alcman's largest surviving fragment is his Maiden Song, or *Partheneion*, discovered in an Egyptian tomb, 1855. The most problematic text of the Greek lyric period, it is riddled with uncertainties ranging from the smallest to the most comprehensive points of interpretation.[44] For this reason, I have not ventured a new translation here. I have, instead, included Mary Lefkowitz's prose rendering (Appendix III), and note, with Hallett (p. 462), the poem's erotic nature: "Here several female chorus members acclaim . . . , one another's outstanding physical qualities graphically and lavishly; here too, they avow in sexually charged language[45] an emotional investment in each other."

Anacreon

According to Pausanias, the first poet after Sappho to make love his principal theme. "Sappho," notes Gerber (p. 222), "can admit that she has often called upon the aid of Aphrodite [§ 1], but the passion she feels is in no way diminished thereby, whereas to Anacreon love is a game which should be entered into only half seriously and with the realization that it will

---

[43]See e.g., § 39, notes.

[44]Notes Gerber (p. 85): "No poem in Greek choral lyric has been the subject of so many different interpretations as Alcman's *Partheneion*, and if the following commentary presents no clear or consistent view, the reason is very simply that I am seldom certain in my own mind of the correct solution to many of the problems involved. I have, therefore, often presented various interpretations without stating any preference."

[45]That is, in equine images; see also §§ 3, 49, 54, 94. Hallett (p. 464) continues by considering the possibility of the Maiden Song as a marriage hymn "delivered by the girls whose own nuptials are imminent to honor the wedding of a 'fellow debutante.'"

never remain constant."[46] Gerber further cites Anacreon for poetic technique more than for subject matter: "His short, compact, stanzas have a limpid grace and exquisite charm, and are completely devoid of excess verbiage, vague imagery or complicated grammar."

For all of this, posterity assessed Anacreon as a drunkard and libertine. When one thinks of "wine, women (/boys), and song" in antiquity, it is Anacreon who comes to mind and who, as a court poet (like Ibycus) composing at royal behest, had little recourse to historical, religious, and philosophic concerns. Anacreon's influence on later poets has been the greatest of any ancient Greek lyricist. A whole body of poetry known as *Anacreontics* was composed by various unknown authors from the period of the Roman Empire to Byzantine times.[47]

---

[46]Though Gerber cites *§* 47 as a clear and unequivocal indication of this disposition, I do not think the piece need be taken quite so lightly. The statement seems more to reflect the poet's indecision than inconstancy. Notes Snell (p. 60) of *§* 47: "The unhappy lover describes his state of struggling helplessness by the paradox that he affirms and negates one and the same thing. He depicts a similar experience when he says that Eros forged him with his hammer and bathed him in the cold stream. [*§* 46]"

[47]The *Anacreontics* have been published in volumes as exquisite as the poems themselves, e.g., *The Odes of Anacreon*, Translated by Thomas Moore, with Fifty-four Illustrative Designs by Girodet De Roussy, London: John Camden Hotten, Picadilly, 1896. (Date following the introduction to the Moore-Girodet collaboration. Moore's first edition dated at 1800 in the Stanley trans., p. xiv.) Pages gold-embossed on three sides. Rhymed verse, English translation only. The volume, while including none of Anacreon's own poetry, leaves the impression that the poems are all Anacreon's own. See also *ANACREON:* with Thomas Stanley's Translation, Illustrated by J. R. Weguelin, London: Lawrence & Bullen, Covent Garden, 1893. Rhymed verse with facing Greek texts, followed by the untranslated Greek texts of Anacreon's true poetry. Engaging introduction traces the *Anacreontics'* manuscript tradition and their earliest editors. The *Anacreontics* themselves are unabashedly termed as "elegant trifles" (elsewhere, the "shallow elegance of the *Anacreontea*"); and Thomas Moore is taken to task for his "flashy renderings."

27

Ibycus

The reader of Greek, no less than of Greek in a quality translation, may readily agree with Campbell's assessment (p. 306) that the rich language and vivid imagery of §§ 91 and 94 set them among the finest examples of Greek poetry. (The present volume, incidentally, had its genesis in those two pieces.) They are the only surviving examples of Ibycus' love poetry. The poet, according to Cicero, excelled in this genre to the point of surpassing Alcaeus and Anacreon. Though we have numerous references to Ibycus' narrative poetry, only a single fragmentary example survives (some 45 verses). In this genre, Ibycus appears to have handled epic/mythological themes (Heracles, the Argonauts, the Trojan War) with an idiosyncrasy owed perhaps to Steisichorus.[48]

Sappho

Sappho's Lesbos, well-wooded, well-cultivated and well-populated lay within several hours of Sardis, the sophisticated capital of the wealthy kingdom of Lydia (§§ 4.19; 8.6; 27; 48.4, notes). The island was active in 7th century trade and colonization; it was torn by bouts of factionalism and political upheaval to which the aristocratic Sappho was sometimes prey (§ 28, notes), though her poetry reflects little of this (note 62, below). The women of Lesbos were famed for

---

[48]The first great poet of *Magna Graecia* (i.e., the Greek settled part of Southern Italy and Sicily); contemporary with Sappho and Alcaeus. Though considered in antiquity the "most Homeric" of poets, he often departed from Homer and Hesiod in the details of his mythology. Ibycus is the second great poet of *Magna Graecia* (before leaving for the court of Polycrates on Samos) and appears to have had his *floruit* some twenty-five years after Steisichorus' death.

28

their beauty (*Il.* 9.129-130, 664) no less than for their sophistication. Beauty contests were a yearly occurrence (§ 26.19, notes).

Ancient criticism of Sappho finds its consensus in her unrivaled poetic supremacy. In epigrams from the *Palatine Anthology* she is regularly counted as tenth of the Muses. "Memory herself was astonished when she heard the honey-sweet Sappho, wondering whether mankind possessed a tenth Muse."[49] Sappho is deemed "the equal of any god" and the *dernier mot* of her craft: "You have established the beginning and end of all lyric song." Plutarch also counts Sappho among the Muses and elaborates: ". . . Sappho utters words truly mingled with fire and gives vent through her song to the heat that consumes her heart." In so doing, she is said to "heal the pain of love with the Muses' melody." Again, in the *Palatine Anthology* she is considered "sweetest of love-pillows to the burning young," a companion to Hymen, god of weddings, at the bridal bed, and to Aphrodite lamenting Adonis in the sacred grove of the blessed.[50]

Sappho generated derision as well as praise in antiquity -- derision, when the concern was more with her sexuality or morality than with her poetry. An important source on the matter is the poet Ovid who, in espousing both sides of the issue, does little to resolve it. At *Tristia* 2.365 Ovid says, "What did Sap-

---

[49]Memory, a wife of Zeus and mother of the Muses. The account of the Muses' birth appears in Hesiod's *Theogony* 1-115.

[50]The reference is to Adonis, son of Cinyras (cf. *§* 40.71), king of Cyprus, by an incestuous union with his daughter (Ovid, *Metamorphoses* 10.298-559, 708-739). Beloved by Aphrodite for his exceptional beauty, and identified with both her and Eros in cult. See further note 59, below, with Friedrich pp. 69-71 and Grigson pp. 55-62.

pho of Lesbos teach but how to love maidens? Yet Sappho herself was safe."[51] (*Lesbia quid docuit Sappho nisi amare puellas/tuta tamen Sappho?*). By *tuta* "safe" Ovid apparently means that Sappho espoused, but herself took no part in, homosexual relations -- a matter of "theory vs. practice."[52] The *Tristia* reference, appearing to exonerate Sappho, is at variance with the *Sappho-Phaon Epistle* (*Heroides* 15.15-20):

Not Pyrrha's coterie nor Methymna's girls
  beguile me now, nor any Lesbian maiden.
Dazzling Cydro's of no account -- Anactoria
  and Atthis, once embraced, are now disdained;[53]
and the hundred others, loved to my reproach,
  relinquish this their claim to callous you alone.[54]

---

[51]*Tristia*. Five books of poems addressed to the emperor, Ovid's wife, and other unnamed persons at Rome. These highly autobiographical materials were written from Ovid's exile at Tomis on the Black Sea and are somewhat monotonous in tone due to the poet's preoccupation with the miseries of banishment.

[52]And, it would seem, a difficult position to maintain (cf. further p. 39, below). From what evidence we have, comment on the nature of Sappho's relationships with women does not begin until Hellenistic times and may derive from 5th century Athenian social, moral and cultural attitudes. See Dover, 1978, pp. 174, 182.

[53]Pyrrha is located in central Lesbos; Methymna, on the northern coast. Sappho herself came from Mytilene on the southeastern coast. For Atthis and Anactoria, see §§ 4.15 and 10.

[54]At line 200 of the poem, Sappho invokes the "Daughters of Lesbos whom I have loved to my disgrace" (see further n. 79, below). The *Sappho-Phaon Epistle* is poem fifteen of Ovid's twenty-one *Heroides* (or *Heroines*), and the most famous of the collection. The poems take the form of letters (in elegiac couplets) by famous women (Penelope, Dido, Helen, and others) to their lovers. The poems' wealth of literary reminiscence and sympathetic portrayals of "hearts submissive to the power of love" more than compensate for a certain formality and rhetoricalness of style. The collection is available with facing Latin in the Loeb series: G. Showerman, *Ovid Heroides and Amores* (Cambridge Mass. and London 1963). The *Sappho-Phaon Epistle* was rendered into couplets by Alexander Pope (1707). A translation is given by Haines (pp. 171-197) with a now dated discussion of Ovidian authenticity.

Maximus of Tyre in an equally famous statement takes a more elevated view of the matter. "The love of the fair Lesbian, if it is right to argue from one age to another, was surely the same as the art of love pursued by Socrates. They both appear to me to have practiced the same sort of friendship, he of males, she of females, both declaring that their beloved were many in number and that they were captivated by all beautiful persons."[55] Such attachment would ideally be of a spiritualized, non-physical variety.[56]

We will return to this issue in our discussion of "Sappho in recent criticism." For the moment, however, we may note that much of Sappho's surviving work is ambiguous about what type of love is at stake and is accordingly more significant than if this were clear.[57] The love that Sappho's Aphrodite controls may be heterosexual or lesbian, and both types find expression in Sappho's work and life. The goddess (§ 4) is as responsible for Helen's going to Troy (and her fulfilled love for Paris) as she is (§ 6) for the departure of the poet's friend to Lydia (and the poet's unrequited longing for her). In addition, while virginity is a cherished state (§ 17), it is not to be cultivated (§ 20). Though its loss may be painful (§§ 18, 19, 21), marriage and the handsomeness of the groom find ready praise (§§ 22, 23, 24, 25). The praise is sometimes ribald (§§ 29, 30). Sappho's longest surviving poem celebrates the wedding of Hector

[55]See p. 42, below, for the conclusion of this famous statement and for discussion; also § 10, notes.
[56]So thought Maximus of Tyre (*Philos.* 18.6) though Athenaeus (5.219b-220a) believed that Socrates himself had physical relations with Alcibiades. See further n. 77, below.
[57]See Friedrich pp. 115-117 to which parts of the following are indebted.

and Andromache (§ 26). From what we know of her life, Sappho was married to a wealthy merchant named Cercolas and had a daughter, Cleis (§ 27 and *Heroides* 15.70, below). Sappho is believed to have ended her life in a suicidal leap for unrequited love of the ferryman, Phaon.

This brings us to the most compelling and elaborate of the legends attaching to Sappho, her leap from the Leucadian cliff.[58] According to a character in Menander's *Leukadia*, Sappho "first leapt from the far-seen rock in wild love-chase of the proud Phaon." According to Ovid's *Sappho-Phaon Epistle*, however, the leap was supposed to cure love (*Heroides* 15.163-172), that is, if it did not kill you first.[59] The Epistle concludes with Sappho's intention of "seeking her fate in the Leucadian wave." Excerpts will suffice to indicate Ovid's view of the factors feeding Sappho's despair as well as the piece's highly charged and rhetorical nature.

---

[58]Cape Leucas, a prominent white rock jutting out from Leucas, an island south of Corfu (off the western coast of Greece) above Ithaca, the home of Odysseus.
[59]Kirkwood (pp. 101-102) notes that the story of Sappho's passion for the Adonis-like, mythic figure which was Phaon "probably took its rise from the fact that Sappho wrote poetry to be used at a ritual honoring a year-spirit either identical with or like Phaon." Kirkwood sees the legend as "arising most likely from Sappho's poetry, expanded by comic burlesque in the 4th century [i.e., Menander], and perpetuated by Ovid." See recently D. Sinos, *Achilles, Patroklos and the Meaning of Philos* (Innsbruck 1980), p. 13, for the association with Adonis of a "fundamental vegetal pattern inherent in Hellenic traditions about deities and heroes" and of an "inordinate prolongation of the onset of youth and either the loss or avoidance of maturity." For Aphrodite and Adonis, see J. Boardman and E. LaRocca, pp. 132-133, 142.

Sappho at great length laments her spurned condition, extravagantly elaborating upon both Phaon's beauty and insensitivity (93-104):

O neither yet man nor yet boy, but charmed inbetween,
    O ornament and glory of your time,
return entrusting your beauty to my embrace.
    Ah, take my love though leaving it unreturned.
I write, and my eyes grow ever wet with welling tears.
    Regard the drops that blur these very words.
Resolved though you were, more gracious yet your
    departure with a brief, "Farewell, O Lesbian maid."
No tears did you take, no adoring kisses of mine
    -- no hint had I of sorrow's swift approach --
thus, taking no token of me were you gone, and no
    keepsake of yours, but for this pain, is mine.

The poem contains the *locus classicus* for the idea that Sappho, in contrast to her beloved, was not especially physically graced (31-34):

If spiteful Nature has denied me beauty's grace,
    then balance my genius in beauty's place!
Though my size is slight, I'm famous throughout the world;
    my stature therein achieves its measurement.

This, however, did not prevent Phaon's loving her for her most valued attribute, the gift of poetry. Sappho's recollection is one of ardent bliss (41-50):

When I read my songs you found me lovely enough,
    and vowed that speech thus never graced another.
As I sang, I remember -- lovers remember all --
    my lips surrendered kisses to your stealth.
My kisses won your praise, I pleased in every way.
    But then above all when we labored at love,
My playfulness occasioned unaccustomed joy,
    the resourceful embraces, the whispered jests,
and when our longings cascaded to consummation --
    the deep, deep languor of our wearied limbs.

Their happiness was but an interlude. Sappho views her suffering in the wake of Phaon's departure as the continuation of a traumatic childhood (59-72):

Is my lot to be bitter, as ever from the start,
    and life become uninterrupted pain?
Six birthdays had I counted when my father's bones,
    too early gathered, grew moist beneath my tears --
while my witless brother burned for a harlot's love,
    enduring, with his every loss, debasement.
Thus reduced, he endangers life and limb at sea,
    heedless to regain what heedlessly was lost,
while hating me for the frequent warnings offered him,
    this the return for candor and concern.
And as if I lacked sufficient grounds for endless care,
    a little daughter now usurps my thoughts.
Now add yourself, most recent cause of my distraction
    -- my craft is blown by impropitious wind.

Strabo, in addition to the quote from Menander, cited above, notes an old custom of the Leucadians every year at the sacrifice of Apollo (whose temple was atop the cliff). As an apotropaic, or averting, rite, they would throw some guilty person from the cliff. Flapping birds and feathers were attached to the victim to break the fall, and a large crowd waited in boats below to rescue him and, if possible, carry him to safety beyond the frontier.

What was to have been a curative, but was ultimately a fatal, leap for Sappho later developed into an expiatory offering, a communal scapegoat. Whether the "old custom" practiced by the Leucadians was still practiced in Strabo's time (some 500 years after Sappho) is difficult to say. Curiously, by Servius' time (again some 500 years later) we find an attenuated version of the ritual. Servius, while leaving the purpose of the leap unspecified, speaks of the custom "now in vogue" of hiring people once a year to throw themselves from the cliff into the sea. The notion of hire would seem to indicate little more than some form of entertainment.

The longevity of the myth and the practices associated with it attest to its grip on the popular imagination. The materials in fact have origins in myth and cult which predate Sappho. Indeed, Strabo, in citing the passage from Menander, denies that Sappho was first to make the leap. In a detailed and far-ranging analysis, Gregory Nagy penetrates the Sapphic exterior of the myth to suggest that the leap has cosmic significance. I summarize and simplify the detailed argument.[60]

Aphrodite first leapt in love for the dead Adonis, and later, in love for Phaethon, son of the Sun-God. The names Phaon/Phaethon are related in Greek and mean "bright." We recall from the tale popularized by Ovid (*Metamorphoses* 1.741-2.400) that Phaethon attempted to drive his father Helios' chariot and, in so doing, to become the Sun himself. He lost control of the chariot and plunged into the sea. Aphrodite, in her astral guise of Evening Star (i.e., the planet Venus = Hesperus, which always sets after sunset) dives daily after the sinking sun (= the falling Phaethon) in order to retrieve him the next morning in the form of Morning Star (also the planet Venus = Heosphorus, which always rises after sunrise). Aphrodite thus pursues the sun at night and is pursued by him at daybreak as she brings the new day on.[61] Sappho then is vicariously projecting her identity onto the god-

---

[60]See esp. Nagy, pp. 173-175.

[61]Nagy cites, in this connection, *S* 1.21 ("For if she flees at first, she'll soon pursue") as an instance of the *amor versus* theme which haunts Sappho.

dess Aphrodite herself. By loving Phaon she becomes
parallel with Aphrodite who loves Phaethon. Such anal-
ogy between Sappho and Aphrodite is, then, the mythic
counterpart to that close association between the two
apparent everywhere in Sappho's poetry. Aphrodite is
Sappho's special goddess, "a cosmic affirmation of
Sappho's own eroticism."[62]

SAPPHO IN RECENT CRITICISM

> Even as early as 1955 a Cambridge professor
> of Greek, Denys Page, had still to demolish
> this blarney of the scholarly moralists who
> refused to recognize that Sappho, and the
> Greeks, and Aphrodite as well, knew more
> than they did about the kinds and inclusive-
> ness of sex, and were honest about it.
>
> G. Grigson

Since approximately the beginning of the present
century, discussion of Sappho has centered on two
issues: the social setting, or context, of her poetry
and the poet's own sexual "preference." As the first
issue has, especially in the last two decades, been
more sensitively and sensibly addressed, the latter
has become more the non-issue. In the present more
sexually permissive age, the poet's passion largely
becomes a given, needing little explanation or apol-
ogy. The inspiration, purpose, and expression of that
passion render the issue of preference as non-existent
as is much of Sappho's own poetry. As Robert Bagg has
noted (p. 47), any shame which the issue of Sappho's
sexuality might cast upon her poetry does not rise

---

[62]Stigers 1981, p. 57. According to Friedrich (p. 108), the
almost totally apolitical nature of Sappho's poetry signals an
analogy between the poet and Aphrodite among the contentious
gods.

from the poems themselves, "which are too frank and healthy to comfort any attempt to degrade them. It comes from those whose restricted sympathies are allowed to choke their pleasure in poetry."

In discussing the social context, or setting, of Sappho's poetry, the great classical scholar U. von Wilamowitz-Moellendorff early fixed -- indeed, fixated upon -- the idea that Sappho was a "headmistress" running some kind of boarding school for girls ("Mädchenpensionat"). The idea, as so many of Wilamowitz's, carried the unquestioned allegiance that his name alone commanded. Though this same idea continues to surface from time to time,[63] it has, in recent years especially, undergone increasing qualification and refinement. We may, indeed, speak of Sappho's "circle." But it is no longer as fashionable to speak of that circle as a *thiasos*: a quasi-religious "college" (band, group, association etc.) devoted to the cult of Aphrodite and the Muses, with Sappho as "priestess," director, and chief personality binding her young devotees together with ties of intimacy and dedication.[64]

---

[63]Both Campbell (p. 261) and Gerber (p. 161) treat it as a possibility.

[64]See Roche, p. xvi, for the formulation (quotations in the text provided) and discussion. West (p. 324) notes that the word *thiasos* appears neither in Sappho nor Alcaeus; "Sappho instead uses the word *hetairai* ["companions"] to connote a close bond between individuals -- a bond which conveys the relationship in which one sleeps on another's bosom. [*§* 33]" Likewise, C. Calame (I, pp. 367-369) who notes that the Sapphic circle and female lyric choirs of Archaic Greece had analogous functions: both consisted of young girls bound to their leader (who acted both as choral leader and educator) through ties defined by the term *hetaira* ("companion"), both found in song and dance their primary activity (see further p. 40, below). J. Russo, however (pp. 721-722), upholds the idea of a *thiasos* with reference to "the sense of the language of Sappho's poems." *Contra* C. Segal (p. 141 with n. 4). Much in this debate depends on how one defines, and envisions the activities of, a *thiasos*.

37

Charles Segal (pp. 141, 145), in pointing to the highly ritualized form, expression and situation of Sappho's poetry, eludicates its actual social function: §§ 1, 3 (invitation to the goddess) and §§ 6, 8 (departure of a companion from the group) present ritualized situations. Ritualized form and expression are apparent, in Segal's formulations, in the "magical,"[65] "incantatory," "charming," "enchanting" (*thelctic*, in the active sense), or "therapeutic"[66] effect produced by 1) recurrent sound patterns, 2) lulling rhythms, and 3) simple sentence repetition (as in § 1.21-24, which "almost seem to assure the success of a spell-bound promise").[67] These effects are especially apparent in the epithalamia, or "wedding songs" (§§ 17, 19,

---

[65]Bagg (p. 63) speaks of Sappho's poetry as magic, "in the sense that convincing someone without the aid or against the wishes of logic is a magical accomplishment. Sappho's personality and voice were capable of staging such events as the arrival of Aphrodite [*§* 1] or communion with a friend over waters. [*§* 8]"

[66]Bagg (p. 74) discusses Sappho's lyrics as "healing enterprises, linguistic attempts to spirit the mind suffering from desire or separation away, into a more satisfactory or pleasurable awareness, drawing upon the medicinal properties of daydream, memory, sensuality, Aphrodite and metaphor to accomplish this." See *ibid.*, p. 49, for "the rhythm and laws of sexual tension [which] underlie several of Sappho's poems." Bagg's idea of "spiriting the mind . . . away etc." is of a kind with Stigers' conception of the Sapphic poem as a "private space" (1981, pp. 59-60): "So the poem [*§* 6] becomes the container of shared memories, hence itself the private space, the common world into which either can enter and find the other imaginatively. . . . The private space is the most important metaphor for love in the poetry of Sappho."

[67]Segal's close scrutiny of sound and rhythmic patterns shows to what extent there is no substitute for the original. For a small example of what is involved, see pp. 15-16, above, and Friedrich, p. 121.

21, 23, 25), poems "closer to public statement and to social situation."

Finally, "her [Sappho's] dexterity and wit in evoking the love-goddess [in § 1] attests to her mastery of love's violence. The ritualized structure of the poem makes the mastery available and aesthetically comprehensible to others. Whatever its origins, the experience becomes a social act. It is embodied in language and song. Others can participate in it. Indeed, the mastery of love which the poem implies -- whether actual or desiderated -- becomes repeatable and accessible to the poetess herself on other occasions."

"Whether actual or desiderated" -- a key distinction, and one reminiscent of Ovid's passing claim to the effect that Sappho taught girls to love but was herself "safe." But criticism of recent decades little looks to Ovid's judgmental formulation. The issue is not clear-cut: "did she or didn't she?" Rather, if she did -- and there is little inclination to argue the contrary (see n. 79, below) -- what was the nature and extent of such activity?

The issue generates responses of varying committedness. "Needless to say," notes Segal (p. 141), "the presence of Aphrodite would not inhibit the expression of love among members of this [Sappho's] community." According to Martin West (pp. 329-320), "Sex was for her [Sappho] the private expression of a total romantic love that had its place in the context of semipublic and public gaiety and song. In this gaiety and

love lay her abiding happiness."[68] For Claude Calame
(I, pp. 430, 438), homosexual relations within the
Sapphic circle were pedagogic in nature, but limited
in practice to Sappho and a single beloved. As for the
others in the circle, the capacity in Sappho's lan-
guage of "communication collective" would allow them
to feel as participants in propaedeutic homosexual
ties between Sappho and one of their number. By "pro-
paedeutic" Calame means (I, pp. 431, 434) that the
homosexual tie was, for the beloved, a typically ado-
lescent form of sexual initiation (and hence, transi-
tory) to the heterosexual adult values sanctioned by
marriage.[69] Such assessments represent a quantum leap
in attitude from such as David M. Robinson in 1924
(pp. 43-44) who fervently denied (in terms yet mani-
festing dread and condemnation) that "Sappho is a

[68]Given the Byronian title of his article, West's view comes
as no surprise ("The isles of Greece, the isles of Greece! Where
burning Sappho loved and sung," *Don Juan* III, 86). The Victorian
Swinburne held a view both solitary for his age and unmatched in
intensity since (from the work quoted above):

Saw the Lesbians kissing across their smitten
Lutes with lips more sweet than the sound of their lute strings,
Mouth to mouth and hand upon hand, her chosen,
    Fairer than all men;

Only saw the beautiful lips and fingers,
Full of songs and kisses and little whispers
Full of music, only beheld among them
    Soar, as birds soar . . .

[69]We know from Plutarch that in Sparta, the noble women loved
young girls, and from Athenaeus (13.602d) that it was customary
for adult women in Sparta to have intercourse with girls before
their marriage. Calame (I, pp. 434-436) relates the Spartan and
Lesbian practices. J. Bremmer, "An Enigmatic Indo-European Rite:
Paederasty," *Arethusa*, Vol. 13 (1980), pp. 292-293, considers
the Lesbian relationship as the counterpart in female initiation
to the practice of male paederasty in Sparta (for which, *ibid.*
and Dover, pp. 189-190).

woman who has given herself up to unnatural and inordinate practices which defy the moral instinct . . . and harden and petrify the soul." As recently as 1968, J. A. Davison (*From Archilochus to Pindar*, London: MacMillan and Co., p. 226) expressed aberrant concern over the "two special difficulties" which, beyond general problems of interpretation, attached to a consideration of Sappho: 1) "the moral question: is Sappho fit to read?" 2) "the aesthetic question: is Sappho worth reading?" Between those who accommodate and those who condemn there are some who prefer to separate personalities, their alleged preferences and practices, from poetry. So Eva Stigers (1981, p. 48): "Sappho's actual, personal experience in sexual relationships is not in question . . . ; [of interest is] Sappho's imaginative projection of emotional life into aesthetically pleasing, abstract shapes."[70]

Where Segal speaks of Sappho's artistry as a mediation[71] between public, social forms of utterance and Sappho's own experience, Bagg (p. 48) dwells more on the shared intimacy of the circle as a whole: "the intimacy of Sappho's circle seems to have been fervent and exclusive . . . ; the sensitive tensile threads of her personality held the girls in an intimacy; the girls felt each other through Sappho. In several poems

---

[70]Similarly Friedrich (p. 117): "Whether or not Sappho was a practicing lesbian or just passionately attracted to women is superficial compared to the more basic fact that her love must include a woman. Here lesbian love and heterosexual love are combined to contrast with male homosexuality (about which she says nothing and implies almost nothing, probably because of lack of interest)."

[71]Segal does not use the term as such in speaking (p. 155) of "rhythmico-ritualizing effects . . . [which] move between the public, social form of utterance and quieter, more relaxed private moments."

we have a sharp picture of Sappho taking a girl's emotional education in hand,[72] showing her how to read the difficult language of memory, sorrow, moonlight or sexual success and how to answer other girls in it [§§ 6, 8]. From the quality of concern in these poems we can say she created and guaranteed a *community of sensibility*." In developing the idea of such a sensibility, Bagg adduces the well-known comparison made by Maximus of Tyre between the Sapphic and Socratic "circles." "What his rival craftsmen, Prodicus, Gorgias, Thrasymachus and Protagoras were to Socrates, that Gorgo and Andromeda were to Sappho, who sometimes takes them to task and at other times refutes them and dissembles with them just like Socrates."[73] The goal of either circle was to attract and cultivate the love of such youth as were gifted equally with physical, spiritual and intellectual qualities.

That the appropriateness of this comparison may elude us today results from a conventional misunderstanding of "Platonic Love" and of such terms as "lesbian, sapphic and sapphism." A history of the last term is provided by Hallett (p. 451, n. 17):[74] "'Sap-

---

[72]Emotional education within the Sapphic "circle" receives merited emphasis in the discussion by Hallett which follows.

[73]See p. 31, above.

[74]Hallett also provides a brief dictionary survey of the term "lesbian" (p. 452, n. 19):

> Webster's *New International Dictionary*, 3d ed. (Springfield, Mass.: G. & C. Merriam Co., 1947), p. 1418, still gives "erotic" as the chief nongeographic meaning of Lesbian, citing "Lesbianism" in the sense of "female homosexuality" as a "medical term." The *Oxford English Dictionary* (Oxford: Clarendon Press, 1933), 6:207, does not even give a sexual meaning for the word "Lesbian." And both E. Klein, *Comprehensive Etymological Dictionary of the English Language* (Amsterdam, Elsevier, 1971), p. 418, and the *Random House Dictionary of the English Language* (New York:

phism,' according to the *Oxford English Dictionary*
(Oxford: Clarendon Press 1933), 9:105, first appears
in Billings's *National Medical Dictionary* of 1809; a
June 1901 issue of the British medical journal *Lancet*
noted that 'Sapphism' and other vices had been treated
in French but not yet in English novels. The French
view of Sappho as a homosexual owes much of its popu-
larity to the publication, in 1895, of Pierre Louÿs's
Songs of Bilitis.[75] These -- closely following upon
Louÿs's translation of Lucian's *Dialogues of the Cour-
tesans* -- purported to be translations of an ancient
Greek manuscript, the autobiography of a peasant girl
who had belonged to Sappho's homosexual circle and
later became a temple prostitute."

Platonic love, for its part, has been succinctly
defined by W. Hamilton as "a common search for truth
and beauty by two persons of the same sex inspired by
mutual affection."[76] The relationship was ideally non-
physical. As the *Symposium* makes clear (209e-211a),
physical attraction, though the necessary starting
point, remains at the bottom of the aesthetic hierar-
chy: physical beauty, moral beauty, the beauty of

Random House, 1966), p. 822, s.v. "Lesbian," still
list the meaning "erotic" ahead of "pertaining to
female homosexuality."
[75]Available in a Capricorn paperback, New York, 1966, M. S.
Buck, trans.; first English trans. by M. S. Buck, 1928. Hallett
records the immediate denunciation of these poems by Wilamowitz
(see p. 37, above), on the grounds that Sappho was "an honorable
lady, wife and mother," and the influence of the Sapphic legend
on Marcel Proust (contemporary with Wilamowitz). Note Miller-
Robinson (p. 63): "In recent years, Pierre Louÿs in *Les Chansons
de Bilitis* (1895) made Mytilene a Sodom, and Sappho a mistress
of courtesans, and so has interpreted the Lesbian poetess too
pornographically, we believe, yet with lyric charm."
[76]W. Hamilton, *Plato Symposium*: Introduction, Translation,
Notes, Penguin Books, 1951-1975, p. 26.

knowledge, the supreme knowledge whose sole object is absolute beauty. While Plato's Socrates vividly comments on the way physical beauty affects him, he yet remains firmly committed in principle to abstinence from homosexual relations. Moreover, he actively dissuades other males from engaging in physical relations with desirable young men (*Symposium* 216d-219d, *Phaedrus* 236d-241d and 244a-257b). Socrates is, nonetheless, realistic enough to allow for human frailty at the starting point, i.e., when physical attraction is consummated (*Phaedrus* 256c): "But if they [the 'Platonic' lovers] turn to a way of life more ignoble and unphilosophic, yet covetous of honor, then perchance in a thoughtless hour, or when the wine is flowing, the wanton horses in their two souls will catch them unawares and bring the two together who, choosing that part which the multitude consider blissful, will achieve their full desire. And once they have fulfilled this desire, they continue therein, though rarely, since their minds are not wholly intent on the undertaking."[77]

---

[77]Plato is less permissive at *Laws* 7.837c, 841d-e. The extent of Socrates' own homosexual activity is a matter Plato does little to clarify. In antiquity, opinion varied on the nature of Socrates' relationship with Alcibiades. And contemporary discussion of Socrates' sexuality has been as fumbling and apologetic as discussion of Sappho's. R. J. Littman, "The Loves of Alcibiades," *TAPA* Vol. 101 (1970), pp. 270-276, does much to "liberate" Socrates from the moralizing strictures of scholarship. "Given the acceptability and wide practice of pederasty in Socrates' circle, and Socrates' erotic nature, it would be most unusual if he did not engage in it himself. Plato's ambiguity and the abhorrence of Judeo-Christian thought to homosexuality until recently has led modern scholars vehemently to deny that Socrates had homosexual relations." See K. J. Dover, "Eros and Nomos (Plato, *Symposium* 182a-185c)," *BICS* Vol. 11 (1964), pp. 31-42, for social convention and codified law (*nomos*) in the practice of homosexuality in 5th century Athens.

By contrast, Sapphic love, as Bagg observes (p. 49), "did not have idealistic and intellectual aspirations directing it. Sappho's love seems to have been transmutable only into solace and communion and most often remains under the warm eyes of Aphrodite as sexual excitement."[78]

Judith Hallett discusses these issues -- emotional education, solace, communion -- as elements in the institutional affirmation of young girls prior to marriage. Hallett, however (unlike, and independent of, Calame), ascribes no sexual attachment to this education. Sappho (pp. 450-461) is not to be read "merely as a confessional poet who voices private feelings to the female objects of her desire," but rather as a poet with "an important social purpose and public function: that of instilling sensual awareness and sexual self-esteem and of facilitating role adjustment in young females coming of age in a sexually

---

[78]Bagg elaborates (p. 80, n. 10): "Homosexuality was less repressed in the ancient world than in our own age, but it would be a mistake to say that the ancients had no prejudice against consummation of this love. The sacred band was a famous oddity, and the most admired milieu where homosexual love was unashamed and cherished -- the Socratic circle of Platonic love -- depended for its existence on non-fulfilment of these physical desires. For Plato, male homosexual love had as its ideal a rarified, non-physical, intensely exhilarating friendship which moved and was felt in a medium *of ideas.* Philosophy was its natural expression. Female homosexual love, on the other hand, lived in a medium of shared sensuality and sensibility, as Sappho shows us in her poems filled with rose chains falling on soft necks, apple boughs full of sleep, moonlit meadows, bowls full of wine, bodies full of glowing desire or harsh deprivation. Its special poignance was that this love could not fertilize the womb, just as it could not engender philosophical discourse. Men identify with the world of ideas, as Freud argues; women don't; the most natural female communication is through some form of sensual awareness." Such assumptions are not, however, to be taken for granted. See discussion by Lefkowitz, below.

segregated society." In such a society, "young women could not have received sexual attentions from their suitors or hoped to find emotional gratification within marriage itself. They could only have turned to other women to become sensually aware, in order to perform adequately in the role to which their society assigned them and to find the sexual validation that could satisfy their needs. Women were the sole individuals with whom they socialized and by whom they were socialized." As an array of socio-cultural institutions appear to have served this precise function in the male sector of society, "it only stands to reason that Greek society would have similarly institutionalized the sensual education and affirmation of upper-class women."

Hallett, moreover, posits a similar distinction in male, as well as female, social circles between "sensual appreciation and sexual appetite." The Greek religious, artistic, and poetic tributes to the male physical ideal are to be taken as "conventional public gestures [and not as "sexual overtures"] intended to enhance the aesthetic appeal of their objects in a culture which placed a high premium on male physical beauty." So also with Sappho, for whom, as often with her male poetic colleagues, a distinction between person (even the first person of her narrative) and poetic *persona* may well often exist.[79]

[79]Stigers (1979, p. 466), while noting that Hallett's article "has some good claims to consideration," suggests that it underestimates the question of Sappho's poetic *persona* and how, among other concerns (see § 5, notes), "erotic admiration via poetry could be effective if the author dissociated herself from it." Stigers further notes (p. 468) that "the praise of young men was undeniably based on sexual attraction" and that the desire to possess a young man was socially acceptable. The same must, then, be assumed valid among women. A similar view is held by Calame (I, p. 431) who notes the identical educational and

Such distinctions, however, are only ideally maintained, and as Mary Lefkowitz observes (p. 113), criticism often finds it difficult to separate an artist's life from his work and to regard creative art, of whatever kind, as public statement. The dependence of criticism on biography leads to certain stereotyped assumptions about the creative process in men as opposed to the creative process in women. While it is assumed that male artists (literary, musical etc.) apply the full range of their intellectual powers in the creation of their art, the assumptions for female artists tend to be more narrowly defined:

> (1) *Any creative woman is a 'deviant', that is, women who have a satisfactory emotional life (home, family and husband) do not need additional creative outlets.* The assumption behind this assumption is that 'deviance' in the case of women results from being deprived of men -- in other words, women artists tend to be (a) old maids or (b) lesbians, either overt female homosexuals or somehow 'masculine'. (2) *Because women poets are emotionally disturbed, their poems are psychological outpourings, i.e. not intellectual but ingenuous, artless, concerned with their inner emotional lives.* As a result, criticism of two such different poets as Sappho and Emily Dickinson can sound remarkably alike.

social roles of pederasty among men and of homoeroticism in the Sapphic circle. F. Lasserre, for his part (pp. 27-31), sees in "les poèmes reputés érotiques" of Sappho and other lyricists a largely encomiastic significance: "le langage de l'amour se prêtait à la louange poétique en raison de son pouvoir affectif et non à cause de ce qu'il exprimait." Lasserre argues the same interpretation for *Heroïdes* 15.15-19 (p. 30, above), stopping short of v. 20 (lit., ". . . what belonged to many [sc. my love] you alone possess") and omitting mention of v. 200.

Lefkowitz proceeds with criticism of a recent interpretation by John Cody of Emily Dickinson's "I had been hungry all these years"[80] and by Denys Page of Sappho § 2, as "vivid illustration of the special criticism applied to female artists." In the first instance, Cody is taken to task for his analyst's, dream interpretive reading of Dickinson, along canonical Freudian lines, whereby *sexual* hunger is the determining metaphor in a poem that primarily concerns sex. In the second instance, Page is criticized for his reading of Sappho's poem as a direct outpouring of emotion, a reading similar in its way to Cody's approach with Dickinson. Lefkowitz proceeds to dismantle psychiatrist George Devereux's masculine-lesbian/female-castration-complex interpretation, according to which Sappho § 2 describes the sort of anxiety attack which Devereux has frequently witnessed in homosexual patients. It is the self-referential application of biographical prejudice which is responsible for such analysis: "thus biography, itself derived from interpretation of the poems, is in turn re-applied to the poems and affects our interpretation of them."[81]

---

[80]John Cody, *After Great Pain: The Inner Life of Emily Dickinson* (Cambridge Mass. 1971).

[81]Lefkowitz's own analysis of § 2 is largely incorporated into my notes on the poem.

48

τὸ μελιχρὸν αὔχημα Λεσβίων Σαπφώ

Sappho, delectable glory of the Lesbians
                    Lucian

Σαπφοῦς βαιὰ μὲν ἀλλὰ ῥόδα . . .

The flowers of Sappho, few, but roses . . .
                    Palatine Anthology

ἐγὼ δὲ φίλημμ᾽ ἀβροσύναν,   ] τοῦτο καί μοι
τὸ λάμπρον ἔρος τὠελίω καὶ τὸ κάλον λέλογχε.

*As for me, I love the exquisite, . . . This and
yearning for the sun has won me brightness and
beauty.*
                    (Athenaeus 15.687b)

49

III

SAPPHO

§ 1

Appareled in flowered allure, deathless,
deceiver, daughter of Zeus, Aphrodite!
Subdue not, nor destroy, this heart, my lady,
4   with distress.

But come to my side, if ever before
while listening, alert from afar as I cried,
you attended, and came leaving your father's
8   golden door,

drawing lovely sparrows to the chariot's rein
who swiftly drew you down to darkened earth,
their wings awhirl along the way through aether's
12   middle main.

Quickly they arrived, and you, O blessed one,
a smile on your immortal face, were asking
what I suffered this time, why this time did
16   I summon;

And what it was my maddened heart did long
for most. "Whom this time shall persuasion lead
as captive to your love? Who, O Sappho,
20   does you wrong?

For if she flees at first, she'll soon pursue;
the gifts she has spurned, she'll shortly bestow;
the love she flaunts, she'll soon long languish for
24   not wanting to."

Come to my side even now, and free me
from crushing concern. Fulfill whatever
yearnings my own heart would fulfill, yourself
28   my ally be.

§ 2

Equal to the gods does he appear,
   that man who sits close by you,
      hears the sound of your sweet voice
4   -- intently near -

and your delightful laughter. That sight,
   I swear, sets my heartbeat pounding;
      the slightest glance at you puts my
8   speech to flight!

My tongue unhinges, a delicate
   flame slips racing neath my skin,
      I see nothing, am blinded, my ears
12   ring, pulsate,

a cold sweat commands me, dread
   grasps at my heart. More pallid
      than grass, I appear to myself
16   nearly dead.

§ 3

Leaving Crete for this sacred enclosure
   arrive! Here's your pleasing grove
      of apple trees, here altars breathing
4   scents of myrrh.

Roses and shadows in this place abound;
   cold water bubbles neath apple bough
      branches whose shuddering leaves sprinkle
8   sleep to the ground.

Here's a Spring-flowered meadow
   with horses agraze, where breezes
      gently blow [   ]
12   [   ]

Here then [   ] taking, Aphrodite,
   with your exquisite touch admix
      the nectar, golden-cupped, to blend with
16   our festivity.

52

§ 4

Some claim that infantry, cavalry corps,
   or seas decked with fleets are the dark earth's
     fairest sight. But I claim the one
4   you adore.

The fact is apparent, self-evident,
   for Helen, far surpassing all mortals
     in beauty, leaving a husband
8   unmatched, went

sailing to Troy nor showed any remorse
   for dear parents or child. [Aphrodite]
     drove her to follow [obeying love's
12   greater force]

[   ]
   [   ] lightly [   ]
     that makes me think of Anactoria
16   though distant,

whose lovely step I would sooner see
   and face sparkling radiant with light, than
     Lydian charioteers or outfitted
20   infantry.

§ 5

I'm filled with desire to die,
see the dewy lotussed shore
of Acheron [flow by . . .

§ 6

"Honestly, I wish I were dead!"
She was leaving me, tears in her eyes.

Much she said, this most of all:
"Ah, Sappho, what we've been through;
5 I swear, I leave not wanting to."

And I made this reply:
"Be on your way, yet remember me now
and again. You know how

we have cared for you.
10 If not I'd remind you [   ]
of joyous times which we once knew:

of rosewreaths and crocus,
of violets you donned at my side,
necklaces flower-tied

15 [tossed] round your gentle neck;
how you annointed yourself
with [   ] a queen's costly scent

and on yielding beds
gentle [   ]
20 desire [of maidens] spent

and no dance [
no shrine [   ] where
we two were not found

25 No precinct [
                    ] sound
            ] . . ."

§ 7

The stars about the radiant moon
consider their brilliant orbs unsightly
when in her fulness she burns brightly
upon the earth . . .

§ 8

She thought you a goddess,
5 your song her special joy.

Among Lydian women
she now has her praise --
as the rosy-fingered moon,

shaming heaven's stars from sight
10 shines, ocean-enthroned,
over flowers in the night,

over fields where chevril grows lush,
where melilot and roses thrill
to evening's dewy touch.

15 Ever wandering there, yearning
for tender Atthis, she languishes --
her gentle spirit crushed.

§ 9

I loved you, Atthis, once long ago;
a child to me then with little to show.

§ 10

Atthis, now you regard me hatefully;
running off to Andromeda you flee.

§ 11

What country girl
dressed in country style
has turned your head around,
unable to keep
her hemline raised
from sweeping up the ground?

§ 12

Alcaeus to Sappho:

"There is something I'd tell you
but shame [won't allow . . ."

Sappho to Alcaeus:

"If you had a desire for the noble and true
and weren't stirring your tongue in some
    scurrilous brew
then shame would depart from your lowered brow,
you'd not dawdle, but speak your mind somehow."

§ 13

Be yet more severe with Doricha,
let her not boast thus in her pride,
that he came once again for the love
which at first he was denied.

§ 14

Longing floats round
  the beautiful girl,
aflutter beholding the gown,
  to my delight . . .

§ 15

Dica, wreath your hair, weaving garlands
of supple anise with tender hands.

§ 16

Such brilliant beauty as you possess
  makes Hermione's look the less,
most fittingly you compare
  to Helen of golden hair.

§ 17

As the sweet apple reddens atop of the bough
  by the tip at the furthest height,
the pickers forgot it, no they didn't, not quite,
  but just couldn't reach it somehow.

§ 18

As the hyacinth
  on the mountain top,
trampling shepherds didn't see
  the purple flower drop.

§ 19

"Maidenhood, maidenhood,
where go you leaving me?"
"I leave you for good,
you've outgrown my company."

§ 20

Do I yet long for virginity?

§ 21

Hesperus, restoring all that shining dawn
  has scattered far and wide,
You bring the sheep, bring the goat, bring
    every fawn
  back to its mother's side.
5   [Not so the bride --
who leaving home is forever gone.]

§ 22

A bowl of ambrosia had
    there been blended,
for the gods Hermes poured,
    all were attended.

They all raised their cups,
    poured a libation,
wished the bridegroom
    his heart's elation.

§ 23

What likeness, O bridegroom, do you most bear?
To a tender sapling you best compare.

§ 24

May unwed maidens
the whole night long
make you and your
violet-girt bride their song.

5 Awake, spread the call,
to your companions all,
that we such hours keep
as see the songful nightingale sleep.

§ 25

O blessed groom, now your wedding's complete
as you prayed; yours is the girl you've adored
as you prayed; her generous beauty, yours.
And the eyes of your bride are honey-sweet,
5 love's smile on the beautiful face, outpoured;
you are graced with the Cyprian's honors.

Came the herald, Idaeus, swift messenger [
"and of the rest of Asia, imperishable fame.
Hector and his comrades bring a bright-eyed girl
from Holy Thebes, in ships on the salty sea,
5 from Placea's streams -- exquisite Andromache.
Bringing purple robes, ivory, bracelets of gold,
oddly-tooled trinkets, silver cups untold."
Thus the messenger. His father quickly rose;
to his friends, through streets well paved, the
    tiding goes.
10 Ilus' sons bend mules to rapid carriages,
the crowd surges, ascends; women, girls unmarried [
Priam's daughters, apart [and men unwed lead
horses to their carts, and greatly charioteers
[*unknown number of missing verses*]
                             ] like to the gods
15   ] holy, all together
set forth [   ] to Ilium,
the sweet-sounding flute [and lyre] blend.
Castanets clash; clear, sacred, maiden songs
    ascend,
the wondrous echo reaches the skies [
20 throughout the streets [
chalices, bowls, [
mingled frankincense, cassia and myrrh.
elder women calling clamorously,
men's thrilling melody, shouted aloud
25 summons Paon, great archer, great lord of the lyre,
they sang of Hector, Andromache, like to the gods.

§ 27

A flower, golden petalled, is my child,
Precious Cleis, for whom all Lydia . . .

§ 28

She who bore me used to say
that in her youth a splendid sight
was hair adorned in a purple band,
but even better the strands
5 yet yellower than torch's light
wreathed in chapleted flower display.

§ 29

The doorkeeper's feet are fourteen yards long,
his sandals are stitched five oxhides strong,
ten cobblers labored at fitting the thong.

§ 30

Raise the roof higher
  -- sing joy to the groom --
carpenters, raise it,
  give him more room.
Equalling Ares he enters the door,
more duly endowed than you built it for.

§ 31

I know not what I want,
my every thought's a taunt.

§ 32

Beauty is beauty as far as it goes,
a good man's beauty immediately shows.

§ 33

May you find rest
on a maiden's soft breast.

§ 34

Mother dear, no longer
does the loom delight --
sweet Cypris commands,
desire conquers me quite.

§ 35

My heart
was racked by Love --
like mountain oaks
by winds above.

§ 36

Love undoes me again --
dissolver of limbs
bittersweet irresistible
creeping in.

§ 37

You came, calmed my desire,
for you I raged,
my breast, a burning pyre,
is now assuaged.

§ 38

The moon departs the sky,
the Pleiads pass from sight,
midnight's hour slips by,
and I lie alone tonight.

§ 39

Forest
flowered
mountain,
Rhipe,
evening's
breast

§ 40

With longing that dissolves the limbs
casting glances more melting than sleep and death
her sweetness serves no idle whim

Astymeloisa makes me no reply
65 but holding a garland
like a glittering star
or golden shoot
or tender down
   [   ]
70] she has come on luxuriant stride
] the moist charm of Cinyras
which settles on maidens' hair

] Astymeloisa in the host
] people's darling
] winning praise

§ 41

Again sweet Love
through the Cyprian's will
melts and distils
my heart.

§ 42

It isn't Aphrodite
but Eros, wild
as a child at play,
down over the flower tops
5 heading this way --
don't touch them, I pray.

§ 43

Maidens with honey tones
   and voices of desire,
my limbs no more can
   carry me. Ah, but to be
5 above the flowering wave --
   a halcyon, a fearless flier
aloft on winged span,
   a sprightly bird blue as the sea.

§ 44

Mountain peaks and gullies sleep,
  ravines and headlands silence keep,
sleep forests and each quadruped
  that dusky earth has ever bred,
5 sleep mountain beasts and swarming bees,
  monsters in blue chasmed seas,
birds that soar on winged spread.

§ 45

Exquisite Eros I'll not neglect,
I'll praise him, garlanded, flower-decked,
who over gods maintains his sway,
as over creatures of a day.

§ 46

Like a smith --
again Love strikes the hammer's blow,
plunging me
in Winter's torrent as I glow.

§ 47

Again do I love, again love not,
this moment sane, the next distraught.

§ 48

Again tossing his purple ball my way
blond Eros strikes calling me out to play
with a gaily sandaled girl.
But she's of Lesbian pedigree
5 and won't have any part of me
because my hair is grey,
and gapes that some other girl agree.

§ 49

Thracian filly, why cast sidelong glances,
why flee as if I'd lost my senses?

I could easily bridle your head in place,
rein you in; run you round the race.

5 Now grazing in meadows you lightly skip
with no nimble horseman to hug your hip.

§ 50

Boys by my words would be disarmed,
what I say, no less than sing, is charmed.

§ 51

Lad with the maiden's glance,
my wish is but to have you near;
you give me not a chance --
my soul's unwitting charioteer.

§ 52

To Olympus I wing my fragile way
to plead with Eros there,
that a lad no longer will delay
his youth with me to share.

§ 53

I pluck this lyre's twenty strings,
Ah, Leucaspis,
each with your youthful freshness rings.

§ 54

O lad with the lovely face,
another's look makes your heart race.
Your caring mother thinks that she

at home will nurse you constantly,
5 but you [   ] the meadows
of hyacinth, where the Cyprian

tethers her horses after they've run.
In the midst [   ] you darted down
putting hearts in a flutter throughout the town.

§ 55

The season comes round;
Megistes, warm of heart,
is willow-crowned,
with honied wine assumes his part.

§ 56

I hate all who rant
and are given to riot.
Megistes you grant
the repose of the quiet.

§ 57

        ] but extend
Your tender thigh, my friend.

§ 58

Gently, like a suckling fawn, newborn,
affrighted in the wood --
his antlered mother gone, and he, forlorn.

§ 59

In dark leafed bay
and green olive
he quivered.

§ 60

Master, with whom rosy Aphrodite,
blue-eyed Nymphs and conquering Eros play,
whose mountainous empery
enthrones you over all that you survey,
5 I beseech you, come well disposed to me,
kind-hearted, attentive, as I pray
Cleobulus be well advised
and the love I bear him, not despised.

§ 61

Cleobulus I adore
for Cleobulus I rage
on Cleobulus I gaze.

§ 62

Come, lad, let the cup go round
whose fifteen leagues no thirst can sound;
ten ladles of water, five of wine,
revelling, still would I walk a straight line.

5 Come, again, no longer let us pour
amid the din's riotous uproar;
no, let us sing sweet hymns instead,
raising our cups as men well bred.

§ 63

I do not like the speakers
    of strife and tearful war
whenever festive beakers
    are filled and hold no more,

5 I'd rather one who mixes
    fine gifts of love and song
and, wistful, reminisces
    of good times all night long.

§ 64

Bring water, bring wine, my boy,
flowered necklaces bring;
with love would I enter the ring.

*

I who sparred so painfully
can finally lift my head and see.

§ 65

Love's dice hold in store
derangement and din of war.

§ 66

Generous to passers-by,
let one drink who's languished dry.

§ 67

Drunk with love,
again, up the Leucadian rock I go
and dive to the hoary brine below.

§ 68

Love who has seen my chin grow white
wings past gold-guilded in his flight.

§ 69

Listen to me who am old,
maiden fair-haired and gowned in gold.

§ 70

Temples already white,
grey, thinning, hair now slight,
graceless age is my plight,
my teeth have lost their bite.
5 Of life all but bereft,
brief is the sweet time left.

This then do I lament
by dread of Hades rent,
for death is a horrid pit,
10 and hard the path down to it.
Descend, and that descent
is fully infinite.

§ 71

I lie wretched, alone,
lifeless, pierced to the bone,
mercilessly pained,
thus have the gods ordained.

§ 72

By such desire of love possessed,
my eyes beset with thickest mist
gentle spirit stolen from my breast.

§ 73

But desire, dissolving my limbs,
undoes me, my friend.

§ 74

Ah, could I but touch Neoboule's hand . . .

. . . totally keeping yourself,
   and in like fashion I'll forebear.
But if you are so very spurred,
   with bed to all things else preferred,
5 we have at home a girl quite fair,
   now most desiring to be wed;
her looks are quite beyond compare."
   So much she spoke, and this I said:

"Daughter of Amphimedo
10   -- a knowing mother nobly bred --
whom now dank earth conceals below,
   many joys does the goddess grant
young men, aside from the divine;
   of these some one will do just fine.
15 We'll better know the one we want
   in parlance hushed, god-sped, lights low.
As you urge, so shall I go.

You think me eager, in a rush?
But by the gated portico
20   --don't be begrudging, don't say *no* --
I'll put in where the grass is lush.
   Neoboule!? the likes of such
assign to someone else's bed.
   She's overripe, flower-fresh no more,
25 with grace of girlhood long since shed.
   Ever short of what she's lusting for,
she's shown it all, the girl's a whore!

To hell with her, and far from me!
May never ruler Zeus decree
30   that I, possessed of such a cur,
become a neighbor's mockery.
   It's you whom I do most prefer,
You're not a two-faced liar like her.
   She, in a word, is too severe,
35 and many the man whom she holds 'dear.'
   'Haste makes waste,' as often said,
avoid what ill you know is near."

I spoke, she followed as I led
to flowers, where I urged our rest.
40   Enfolded by my cloak outspread
(my hand positioned neath her head),
   she hindered trembling like a fawn,
though I, undaunted, urged her on
   and gently took hold of her breast;
45 soon after was she all undressed.

        Such maiden's charm in that fair skin
    I scarce knew where I should begin --
    I reconnoitered all her frame
    released all my force and fell tame,
50   just touching on the tawny hair . . .

§ 76

With you love's battles to engage,
battle as drink, when thirst does rage.

§ 77

Such did she conspire:
in one hand water; the other, fire.

§ 78

Enyalius, lord of battles, I attend;
the Muses' lovely gift I also comprehend.

§ 79

I knead my bread with spear in hand,
pour my wine with spear in hand,
drinking, aside my spear I stand.

§ 80

I hate the general, heavy set,
    standing feet spread wide,
who most about his beard does fret,
    whose hairdo is his pride,
5 I rather one who's spare and smart,
who walks firm-footed, full of heart.

§ 81

Heart, heart, overwhelmed with confusion past cure,
to adversities bearing your chest, endure.
Stand safely aside from the snare of a foe,
don't, in victory, overexultant grow,
5 nor bested, indoors bemoan your overthrow.
Temper triumph, be not grieving overwrought,
but comprehend the rhythm of mankind's lot.

§ 82

In my shield does some Thracian now rejoice,
which, flawless, I jettisoned, having no choice
were I to escape alive. Let it go to Hell!
Another will serve me no less well.

§ 83

Deference and fame depart the dead,
let life and living be sought instead,
demise holds naught but dread.

§ 84

A fig tree on its rock, feeding many crows,
accessible, loved by all, to all exposed.

§ 85

Like a mating crow,
pleasured, perching low,
poised on a jutting peak,
slack pinioned, sleek.

§ 86

We have a sturdy ox at home,
knows how to plough, need not be shown.

§ 87

Gain gathered by long time and labor
often flows down the gut of a whore.

§ 88

And on that skin, insatiable, alight,
hurling belly on belly, thigh on thigh.

§ 89

Her joy is a myrtle sprig
    and a lovely flowering rose,
her long hair shades her
    shoulders and neck,
all down her back it flows.

§ 90

Breast and fragrant hair
to make even an old man despair.

IBYCUS

for Tamara
A love of mine no season knew . . .

§ 91

In Spring the river streams bedew
the quinces in Cydonia,
where sacred stands the Maidens' grove
and shaded bough vine-blossomed grows;
5 this love of mine no season knows
but races -- northern Thracian blast
from Aphrodite's shrine outcast
ablaze with flash of lightning, black
with shameless fits of parching rage
10 to rack my frame, unceasingly.

§ 92

Tamara daemon of my brain
exquisite torment wreaking cain
with seething song, incarnate fright,
my mind's disruption, mind's delight;
sing stinging strains that lash my brain
refrains of unrelenting pain
until my mind completely flayed
with scourge of siren serenade
will bleed to have you far away
while pleading, stay, Tamara, stay.

§ 93

The murmured chant
"I want you now . . ."
pounds frantically
beneath my brow;
your wanton nails
assail my back
the tightening hold
impales me to the rack,
where bound, torn and tense,
resounding cadence
makes me crack --
a heathen din
a harrowing hymn
to crush my marrow
limb by limb
confound the power
of my will, reduced to dust, these two,
within the mill
and ground with sweat and tears
a mound to spill,
insensate, from the gears
                        of you.

§ 94

Love's melting look from eyes dark-browed
has cast me into Cyprian chains
unfailing, charmed in every wise.
How I shake at his approach!
5 As a horse once winner of the prize
in later years must bear the reins
and cart, unwilling, past the crowd.

IV

NOTES

Notes are intended to provide the reader (1) with brief introductory/background information to all but the most fragmentary selections, (2) with individual points of explanation and/or interpretation (including meanings of key Greek words), and (3) with literal translation (in quotations, preceded by "lit.") where my own rendering is more literary than literal. Where interpretation (beyond the act itself of translating) is involved, my own contribution has been modest. I have deferred, instead, to such varied and capable interpretations as are already on record. In selecting the best of these, I have most often had recourse to the excellent commentaries of Douglas Gerber and David Campbell (including largely the same poems, though not all the poems translated here) and, with the addition of C. M. Bowra and H. D. Rankin, to the studies utilized in the Introduction.

I have attempted as complete a poem cross-referencing as possible to help the reader toward a perception of thematic similarity and contrast between poems and authors. At the same time, I have, in the interest of practicality, been rather selective in cross-references to other Greek and Roman authors (epic, dramatic, etc.). Such cross-references, fully and systematically undertaken, would exceed the interests and needs of readers, most of them encountering the poems for the first time and in English. For the same reason, while I regularly note the author responsible for preserving a poem or fragment, I omit mention (but for exceptional cases, e.g., §§ 1, 2) of the specific work and its section. Most of the authors and works are so obscure as to remain unknown or only vaguely recalled (and never read) by advanced students and teachers of classics, alike. (A brief glossary at the least identifies authors and time periods.) The one exception is Athenaeus whose sole surviving, and highly engaging, work *Doctors at Dinner* preserves far the greatest percentage of all surviving archaic Greek lyric. The parenthesized references following all citations of Athenaeus are to the easily accessible Loeb Classical edition (Greek with facing English translation) by C. B. Gulick. Parenthesized references following my own numberings are to the corresponding number of the critical edition as cited in the bibliography (information of interest to the specialist only).

SAPPHO

§ 1 (1LP)   Our main source for the *Hymn to Aphrodite*, the opening poem in Sappho's nine books of verse, is Dionysius of Halicarnassus (*Literary Composition* 173-179). He cites it as an example of the polished and exuberant style of composition and quotes it in full after the following remark:

> The finished and brilliant style of composition . . . has the following characteristics: . . . It would not be out of place for me to enumerate here the finest exponents of it. Among epic writers I should give the first place in this style to Hesiod, among lyrists to Sappho, with Anacreon and Simonides next to her; among tragic poets there is only one example, Euripides. . . . I will now give illustrations of this style, taking Sappho to represent the poets . . .

1. *Appareled in flowered allure*: In rendering the opening epithet *"poikilothrone"* I have followed

(among others) Michael Putnam, "Throna and Sappho 1.1," *CJ* Vol. 56 (1960), pp. 79-83: "Aphrodite is invoked by Sappho as the goddess whose robe is richly-dight with the charms of love, perhaps in the form of flowers." The epithet occurs only here and is usually rendered to convey some notion of Aphrodite as seated on a decorated throne (see pp. 9-13, above). This meaning, while supported by a number of literary and artistic representations (see Page, p. 5), is as fully congenial neither to the nature of the goddess nor to the tone of the poem, overall -- an idea I was pleased to find corroborated by Farnell's commentary of 1891, *ad. loc.*: "the epithet in this sense ["goddess of the spangled flowers"] would be particularly appropriate from the lips of Sappho, whose love of flowers is conspicuous." The controversy is summarized by K. Stanley, "The Role of Aphrodite in Sappho Fr. 1," *GRBS* Vol. 17 (1976), pp. 309-310, n. 26, who feels "it would be unwise . . . to exclude either translation."

3. *Subdue not, nor destroy, this heart, my lady*: lit., "Do not, I implore you, break my spirit, lady, with *heartache* or *anguish*." The italicized words, similar both in sound and meaning, are hardly distinguishable in Greek (*asaisi/oniaisi*) and are used by medical writers in reference to physical distress.

5. *if ever before*: This is not the first time Sappho has had to call on Aphrodite to help her with un-requited love. The thrice repeated "this time" (verses 15, 18: lit., "again") indicates Aphro-dite's appreciation of the situation and shows her response to be one of playful and sympathetic reproach. (Page, pp. 13-14, argues for reproof and impatience in Aphrodite's words.) In addi-tion, the formulation "if ever before" is humor-ous in its present context. In traditional prayer requests to a divinity, the suppliant can expect a favor in return for services rendered. So with the priest Chryses in *Il.* 1.39-42: ". . . if ever it pleased your heart that I built your temple/If ever it pleased you that I burned rich thigh pieces/Of bulls and goats, then fulfill this wish I pray for:/May your arrows repay the Greeks for the tears I've shed." Sappho's *quid pro quo* is one, not of reciprocity, but of precedent on the goddess' part, as if to say, "You've done it before, so do it again."

7. *father's*: Only in Hesiod (*Th.* 176-200) is Aphrodite born in the sea foam (Gr., *aphros*) from the severed genitals of Ouranos. In Homer and elsewhere she is the daughter of Zeus.

9. *sparrows*: Sparrows were often cited by ancient writers for their lasciviousness and fecundity. Their flesh and eggs might be eaten for their aphrodisiac effect. It is natural, then, that they be pictured as drawing the love-goddess' chariot. (Sparrows appear in the erotic contexts of Poems 2 and 3 -- to "Lesbia" -- of the Roman poet, Catullus.) It seems less natural, however, that Aphrodite should descend in a (war-) chariot, at all. See note on v. 28, below, and Stanley, pp. 312-313, 320, for the militancy which characterizes Aphrodite's epiphany from start to finish ("subdue not . . . my ally be"). That the horses, expected both by context and diction, are replaced by sparrows, "symbolically joins to the idea of strife that of diminuitive charm."

9.- For the marked epic influences in this stanza and
12. their implications for lyric as a whole, see Charles R. Beye, *Ancient Greek Literature and Society* (New York: Anchor 1975), p. 124.

14. *a smile on your immortal face*: One of Aphrodite's traditional epic epithets is "smile- (or laughter-) loving." Hesiod (*Th.* 205-206) lists her domains as "the whispering together of girls, *smiles*, deceits, delight and the sweetness of love, and flattery."

15. *this time* (see note on v. 5, above): The word is often used in erotic verse of love's renewed assault (see § 48.1, note). B. Snell (p. 57) in a discussion of such instances, speaks of Sappho's visualizing her sensations *sub specie iterationis*. We may note that Sappho begins (v. 15) by indirectly quoting Aphrodite in the first three of five questions and then quotes the goddess directly. She thus provides stylistic diversity to what might otherwise prove a cumbersome number of questions if all asked either directly or indirectly. The indirectness of the first three questions is further significant in that Sappho allows her directest and most compelling concerns to be indirectly voiced by Aphrodite. One thus senses Sappho's own awareness of how routine such concerns must by now appear to the goddess.

104

21. *if she flees at first, she'll soon pursue*: Sappho's conquest is of an unwilling lover and contrasts with the grim (and archetypal) chase of Hector by Achilles (*Il.* 22.199-201). For such "converted" instances, see § 2.1, note. The stanza is subject to varying interpretation. Stanley (p. 320) questions Aphrodite's efficacy (as ally of Sappho's amorous battles) in offering only reversal instead of permanent peace. A. Giacomelli, "The Justice of Aphrodite in Sappho, Fr. 1," *TAPA* Vol. 110 (1980), p. 136, notes that "Aphrodite's statements contain no direct object. She does not say that the girl will pursue Sappho . . . For it is not the case generally in Greek poetry that scorned lovers pin their hopes on a mutual reversal of erotic roles. In general, forlorn lovers console themselves with a much less fantastic thought: namely, that the unresponsive beloved will one day grow up and become a lover himself, or herself, and in the role of lover will pursue an unresponsive beloved and will come to 'know what it feels like' to be rejected." This explanation answers Dover's concern (1978, p. 177) that the "obliteration of the usual distinction between a dominant and a subordinate partner is contrary to what the evidence for Greek male homosexuality would have led us to expect."

24. *not wanting to*: The feminine singular participle (*etheloisa*) is the only indication in the poem that Sappho's love is for one of the same sex. Translators long found it convenient to overlook this fact. The turning point came in the 1925 translation by Marion Miller. Writes E. Govett (see Miller-Robinson, pp. 10-11): "His [Miller's] translation of this hymn is unquestionably the best in our language, though this is perhaps partly due to the fact that he is almost the only translator who has adhered to the text in regard to the sex of the loved person." Aphrodite's power is such that it can force the recalcitrant lover to a passion of which she remains disdainful. This heightens both Aphrodite's and Sappho's victory, as the girl's loving "not wanting to" makes her undergo the opposite of Sappho's having loved without, in turn, being wanted. The result would be far less impressive if the two "loved happily ever after." Instead, Sappho's anguish is transferred to the girl who, disdainful all the while, yet gives way to passion. Alternatively,

Giacomelli, p. 139: "So, if the beloved girl in Sappho's poem is to leave behind the role of beloved and take on, properly and completely, the role of lover, this will necessarily involve a coercion of her will. As lover, she will, by definition, find herself acting [*not wanting to*]."

25.- *Come* . . . *free* . . . *fulfill* . . . *be*: All
28. direct commands in Greek. Sappho is no less reluctant to call upon Aphrodite continually than she is to make her demands outright. So also v. 3: *subdue not*, v. 4: *But come*.

28. *ally*: lit., "fellow-fighter." A common metaphor in love-contexts. Aphrodite is expectedly ineffective in battle as seen, for instance, by the wound she suffers at Diomedes' hands in *Iliad* 5. Her efficacy in the battles of love is also questionable (see note on v. 21, above).

§ 2 (31LP)   Longinus (*On the Sublime* 10.1-3) prefaces his quotation of the poem with the following remark:

> For instance, Sappho everywhere chooses the emotions that attend delirious passion from its accompaniments in actual life. Wherein does she demonstrate her supreme excellence? In the skill with which she selects and binds together the most striking and vehement circumstances of passion.

After quoting the poem, he goes on to comment:

> Are you not amazed how at one instant she summons, as though they were all alien from herself and dispersed, soul, body, ears, tongue, eyes, color? Uniting contradictions, she is, at one and the same time, hot and cold, in her senses and out of her mind, for she is either terrified or at the point of death. The effect desired is that not one passion only should be seen, but a concourse of passions. All such things occur in the case of lovers, but it is, as I said, the selection of the most striking of them and their combination into a single whole that has produced the singular excellence of the passage.

106

On the inadequacies of Longinus' appraisal, see Page, p. 27; on the inadequacies of Page's, Lefkowitz, pp. 118-119. The poem was freely translated by Catullus (Poem 51). The view (now outmoded) long prevailed that the poem was sung at a wedding and that the man in the opening verses was a bridegroom. More to the point is the narrator's feeling and perspective, on which Lefkowitz has incisively commented: "It is important to remember that what she [the narrator] is describing is an illusion, 'he seems to me' . . . , 'I seem to myself' . . . . The time is indefinite, the illusion happens over and over: 'whenever I look at you' . . . . The man has no specific identity; he is 'whoever . . . sits opposite.' The exaggerated terms in which the narrator's reactions are described add to the sense of illusion: the broken tongue, the sweat that grasps, the shuddering . . . , and being greener than grass do not portray the condition of the narrator in real life." Though the situation be illusion, it is no less excruciating for Sappho's complete exclusion from it by a rival (i.e., a male) she cannot meet on his own terms or replace in the girl's affections. This is not to accuse Sappho of "penis envy" as interpretors with a psychological bent have done. Says Lefkowitz (p. 121), "What the man has that she (the narrator) doesn't have . . . is not male generative capacity but physical strength; he seems 'like the gods' while she is faint and powerless." Though I much agree with Lefkowitz's interpretation, I cannot go quite so far as she in excluding jealousy as a part of the narrator's reaction.

1. *Equal to the gods:* or "like the gods." Lefkowitz (pp. 121-122) cites this as one of several instances in which a Homeric formula is "converted" from the context of war to the struggles of emotion. "It is as if Sappho were saying that what happens in a woman's life also partakes of the significance of the man's world of war." This equivalence is also apparent in the last two stanzas of § 4.

3.- *hears the sound . . . delightful laughter*: "Since
5. it is precisely the intonations of speech and laughter which, by appearing to a jealous person to betray an unexpected intimacy between two other people, act as a detonator of intolerable emotional stress" (Dover 1978, p. 178).

7.   *the slightest glance*: lit., "for whenever I look
     at you briefly." The "I" of the poem "glances
     frequently and repeatedly at the girl in the wild
     hope of disproving by sight the inference she
     drew from sound, but that inference is only con-
     firmed" (Dover 1978, p. 178).

9.   *My tongue unhinges*: Sappho's helplessness is com-
     plete. For a poet in a basically oral culture, to
     lose the power of articulation is to lose the
     essence of identity.

14.- *more pallid/than grass*: ". . . translates the
15. Homeric 'green fear' for one's life in battle
     into the context of daily existence" (Lefkowitz,
     p. 121). Clearly *pale* grass (i.e., unwatered,
     withered) is at issue, as the following words
     suggest.

15.- *I appear to myself/nearly dead*: In v. 1 Sappho
16. relates how the man "appears" to her. In react-
     ing, she comes full-circle to how she "appears"
     to herself. (In the Greek, "appear" is the first
     word of vs. 1 and 16.) The sense of illusion
     framed by these two "appearances" is "one of the
     first expressions of what will later become one
     of the primary concerns of poetry and philosophy:
     the effects of the imagination" (Lefkowitz, p.
     122). The full expression "I appear . . . dead"
     is idiomatic in Greek, lit., "I appear to my very
     self needing of little to die."

          The near finality of death and the balance
     with "appear" would seem to bring the poem to a
     close at v. 16. But such is not the case. Longi-
     nus continues with an only partially comprehensi-
     ble verse: "But everything is endurable, since
     even a poor man . . ." Longinus might have
     stopped when he realized the stanza no longer il-
     lustrated his reason for quoting (Gerber, p.
     170). Catullus' version of the poem has a fifth
     stanza on the ruinous consequences of sloth (*oti-
     um*). Beyond the note of shared self-admonition,
     the stanza would appear to diverge completely
     from its Sapphic predecessor. Equally divergent
     are the conjectures concerning Sappho's subject
     matter in the fifth stanza: ". . . any change
     that is to come about must take place through en-
     durance. As a woman, she [Sappho] must rely on
     the special weapons of the oppressed, miracles
     and patience" (Lefkowitz, p. 121). ". . . the man

who appeared 'equal to the gods,' and was displaced from our attention at once by his companion, is sharply recalled by the warning that prosperity may collapse if God so wills. The tables may be turned" (West, p. 313). ". . . The obvious completion of her line of thought is that she must brace herself to bear all the symptoms that batter her in the girl's presence, *because she means to enter that presence, to bear the obliterating proximity*" (Wills, p. 190). (West [pp. 312-314], on the basis of shared phraseology and theme in the poet Theognis, reconstructs Sappho's stanza with the following sense: "But no thing is too hard to bear;/for God can make the poor man rich,/or bring to nothing one who seems blessed." West notes that this idea shares the same optimism as § 1.21-24.)

§ 3 (2LP) Written on a potsherd in a hand assigned to the 3rd century B.C., and therefore one of the two oldest surviving remnants of the text of Sappho. The only lyric fragment thus preserved. First published in 1937. Page (p. 35) notes: "There is no distinction between lines in the stanza; at the ends of the stanzas themselves a small space is left vacant. The text is remarkably corrupt, though the hand is surely a fluent and practiced one; the writer was either very careless or very ignorant, or both." Campbell (p. 267) refers to an "uncomprehending copyist." A series of poems might be written on sherds, with one .poem spread over more than a single sherd (see Page, p. 36, n. 1). Verses 5-8 were known from Hermogenes, verses 13-16 from a version in Athenaeus (11.463e).

1. *Leaving Crete*: Aphrodite stepped out of the sea on the western coast of Cyprus, at Paphos (see § 1.7, note). Though Diodorus observes that the Cretans claimed Aphrodite was first worshipped on their island, the goddess' association with Crete remains problematic (see West, p. 316). Sappho summons Aphrodite to a temple to join her and her companions in some public festivity. In § 1, Sappho summons the goddess for purely personal reasons.

2. *Your pleasing grove*: Bowra notes (p. 197) that Sappho, "in making her hymn tell of the place where the rite is to be held, suggests to the goddess that it is well suited to her different

functions and implies that at such a place and in such a season, she will enjoy a proper welcome." See also the notes to vs. 3 and 10, below.

3. *apple trees*: The apple is an erotic fruit both in Greek and Roman literature and is one of Aphrodite's emblems. See §§ 3.6; 17; 48.1, note; and Stigers 1977, n. 17, for bibliography. At Magnesia (on the northeastern coast of Greece), Aphrodite was worshipped as "Aphrodite of the Apples" (see Bowra, p. 197, n. 4). The fruit in question may equally be a quince; see § 91.

8. *sleep:* As Campbell notes (pp. 267-268), not just sleep (Gr., *hypnos*), but deep sleep (Gr., *koma*) induced by enchantment or other supernatural means -- here by the bubbling water and rustling leaves.

10. Because of their vitality and grace, horses often come to mind in erotic contexts. See especially the detailed comparison of Paris to a horse after a sexual encounter with Helen (*Il.* 6.503-514), and §§ 49, 54. In § 94, the horse is decrepit and broken down. But unlike the horses in such contexts, the horses which appear in Sappho's poetry are "associated with men, implicitly dissociated from women" (Stigers 1979, p. 469). For such special associations in Sappho's language, see further § 7, notes.

14. *exquisite*: Gr., *abros*, a favorite word of Sappho's; the essence and process of Aphrodite. See §§ 26.5, 45 and p. 49, above. For the range of the word in Greek, see G. Nagy, pp. 176-177, and W. Verdenius, *"ABROS,"* *Mnemosyne*, Vol. 15 (1962), pp. 392-393, who notes the basic underlying meaning of "ripeness," of "being in the flower of youth." Thus the adverb: "luxuriantly."

13.- Aphrodite is thought to be among the celebrants.
15. "The earthly occasion has a divine significance" (Bowra, p. 198). The poem most likely did not end here as Athenaeus continues with words that are a probable prose paraphrase of the beginning of another stanza. We should, as Page suggests (p. 39), expect Sappho to proceed to give some reason for her invocation of the goddess.

§ 4 (16LP)   The poem is preserved on papyrus. Sappho sees her own feminine ideal against the mas-

110

culine ideal of such as delight in a military display. For this opposition, see J. D. Marry.

3.- *the one/you adore*: lit., "that, whatever it be,
4. which one loves." The Greek conveys a comprehensive range of possibilities.

6. *Helen*: For other poets Helen of Troy served as a warning or object of condemnation. For Sappho, notes Bowra (p. 181), "the story of Helen is not . . . a warning, but an example, readily understood, of the power of love to break familiar bonds and force its victims to risk everything for it. Sappho makes it the center of her life, because it is not only radiant and enthralling but in the end irresistible." E. S. Stigers (1981a) observes that the poem describes Helen "as the most beautiful and as making the choice about what is most beautiful." Stigers draws significant comparisons on the consequences of love within the sphere of the human (Sappho), semi-divine (Helen), and divine (Aphrodite). My thanks to the author for providing me with a typescript of her paper.

7. *a husband/unmatched*: The reference is to Menelaus who, if truth be spoken, receives a largely mediocre portrayal throughout the *Iliad*. Moreover, his brother, Agamemnon, is leader of the Greek host, though it is Menelaus' wife they are fighting for. When Helen and Menelaus appear together in *Odyssey* 4, Menelaus is decidedly upstaged and made to look the dullard by his wife. As we learn from the Hesiodic *Catalogue of Helen's Suitors* Menelaus got Helen by offering the most bountiful gifts (see Evelyn-White, p. 199).

9. *nor showed any remorse*: At *Il.* 3.139-140, and 15.662-663, however, Helen is filled with self-reproach and longing for her family and native Sparta. Helen and Menelaus' children were Hermione (see § 16) and Megapenthes ("great suffering"); see *Od.* 4.4ff.

17.- Sappho finds the mere approach and radiance of
20. Anactoria more irresistible and awe-inspiring than the advance of armies in full panoply. Page (p. 57) fully misses the point: "The idea may seem a little fanciful: but this stanza was either a little fanciful or a little dull." The

Lydians were known as a particularly powerful and splendid race. See §§ 8 and 27.

§ 5 (95LP)   Preserved on papyrus as vs. 11-14 of a sixteen verse fragment. In the beginning, Sappho apparently relates that her life has become unhappy, whereupon the god Hermes appears. In a new interpretation by D. D. Boedeker, "Sappho and Acheron" in *Arktouros: Hellenic Studies Presented to Bernard Knox* (Berlin 1981), p. 52, "Sappho clearly recalls well-known epic motifs concerning death and the afterlife, and then reverses her audience's expectations [cf. also § 26, notes] . . . : the narrator *refuses* the offer of Hermes [of 'exaltation'], *desires* rather than fears a transition to the world of death, and imagines a Hades of fertility and tranquility. The poem becomes a new, personal statement of values, a denial and reshaping of epic-heroic ideals. The end result is one that only she could envision: a death that nurtures, an Elysian Acheron." Stigers (1979, p. 466) speculates whether Sappho's reiterated wish to die (see also §§ 2.15, 6) would not appear ill-omened in the public celebratory setting or rite of passage for which Hallett (1979) argues.

2. *dewy lotussed shore*: "Lotus, first, implies the fertile beauty of flowers and the easy nurture of fruit effortlessly gathered. . . . The *lethe* [forgetfulness] induced by the Odyssean lotus [*Od.* 9.83-103] may well have influenced Sappho's choice of plant in this setting: not only is her Acheron floral and fertile, perhaps it also nurtures oblivion to the cares which motivate the desire for death" (Boedeker, p. 48). See *ibid.* for the fertilizing role of dew and Grigson, p. 197, for the lotus' connection with birth, sun, and life.

§ 6 (94LP)   Preserved on a 6th century parchment and published for the first time in Berlin, 1907. The same parchment contains § 8 and several other scraps. Sappho's theme is the departure of a friend whom she reminds of happy days spent together. "The poem preserves the moment when Sappho transmutes the old, physical closeness into a new purely emotional connection. So the poem becomes the container of shared memories, hence itself the private space . . . [where]

either can enter and find the other imaginatively" (Stigers, 1981, p. 59).

1. *Honestly*: lit., "undeceitfully" (Gr., *adolos*). Deceit (*dolos*) is one of Aphrodite's trademarks, as when Sappho addresses her as "Deceiver" (§ 1.1: Gr., *doloploke*, lit., "weaver of deceit"). Understood in this way, the term conveys more than the everyday English expression, "honestly." It indicates the sincerest love from which love's most treacherous quality, deceit, is absent. The language, then, is suited to Aphrodite while designating a pain that is genuine. The first verse is assumed to be Sappho's, though it could be that of her departing friend. *I wish I were dead*: "The wish to die, as often in Sappho, is a metaphor for the rejection of present time, and memory, that tomb where the present lies when it has died, may serve as a surrogate for physical death" (T. McEvilley, "Sappho, Fragment Ninety-Four," *Phoenix*, Vol. 25 [1971] p. 8).

4. *Ah, . . . what we've been through*: lit., "how terribly we've suffered." The Greek verb *pascho* "to suffer" always indicates something bad. Its use here injects a retrospective note of pain into joys previously shared, as those joys are now contemplated at the moment of termination. ("The loss now gripping both women, . . . cannot be separated from the loss and suffering which cling to all sweet and satisfying moments," Bagg, p. 58.) The same ambivalence is evident in vs. 10-11: lit., "if not, I would remind you of such lovely things as we have *suffered*." Commentators are curiously reticent on this point.

7.- *Be on your way, yet remember me now/and again*:
8. lit., "go, and farewell, and be mindful of me." The phrasing in Greek recalls situations in Epic where females are forced to reconcile themselves to their lover's, or would-be lover's, departure. See respectively *Od.* 5.204-205 (Calypso to Odysseus) and *Od.* 8.461-462 (Nausicaa to Odysseus).

0. *[of maidens]*: Only the last five of the eight Greek letters are clear. Bowra (p. 191) supplies the full word in his printing of the Greek text. Page (p. 80) contends on papyrological grounds that "all we can say is that it [the word] is not 'maidens.'" Campbell and Gerber are silent. "The appealing restoration," notes McEvilley (p. 3),

113

"strengthens a suggestion which, even without it, is amply strong," since Sappho uses *apalos* (vv. 16 and 19, "gentle") elsewhere predominately to describe girls in erotic situations. That the girl, to judge from the verb form, appears to be satisfying *someone else's* desire (Stigers 1979, p. 468; Dover, p. 176) is a moot distinction. The passage seems clearly to refer to a homosexual act and is the only such reference in Sappho's surviving poetry. (A fragmentary lyric [99LP], sometimes ascribed to Sappho, sometimes to Alcaeus, contains part of a word -- *olisbos* -- meaning artificial phallus. The broken context, however, allows no inference as to the object's use or the poet's stance toward it. See Hallett, p. 453, Kirkwood, pp. 269-270, Page, pp. 144-145.)

§ 7 (34LP)   Quoted by Eustathius in his commentary on *Il.* 8.555. E. Stigers (1979, p. 470) sees in her use of the moon, both in this and the following poem, Sappho's intention of connecting women with "the mysterious rhythms of the moon as separate from the sharp, bright male world of sun and stars."

§ 8 (96LP)   From the same parchment as § 6. Both are poems of departure or absence. Sappho comforts Atthis (see v. 16 and §§ 9 and 10) by assuring her that another girl, now in Lydia, has not forgotten her. The greater part of the poem is occupied by Sappho's most expansive surviving simile. The poem begins after three broken lines and trails off into nineteen highly fragmentary lines.

8.   *rosy-fingered moon*: A phrase which has occasioned much puzzlement. Homer often uses the expression "rosy-fingered dawn": the rising sun streaks the sky with rosy rays, or "fingers." How this same expression might apply to the moon is discussed with no satisfactory solution, by Page (p. 90 and Campbell (p. 280). See also Kirkwood, pp 253-254, for conjectures and bibliography. Friedrich (pp. 113-114) notes the usage as "an extraordinary symbol that combines a reddish dusk, a transformation of a setting sun into a rising moon, an erotic condensation of Lesbian love play, and perhaps, an experiment with a new, woman's language." This last suggestion is much in the spirit of Stigers, as quoted in § 7, notes.

8.- *as the rosy- . . . dewy*: lit., "like the rosy-
14. fingered moon after sunset, surpassing all the
stars, its light spreads over the salty sea and
the fields of flowers; and the dew descends
abroad in beauty, and roses, tender chevril and
flowery melilot bloom."

15. *Wandering*: lit., "going, pacing to and fro."

15.- We return to the girl after a simile which "has
17. gone so far beyond its starting point, that the
girl is, for the moment forgotten." So Page (pp.
94-95), who also notes "the principal attempts,
all unsuccessful, to define a delicate relation-
ship between the simile and the theme, between
the description of the natural functions of the
moon and the consolation of Atthis or the beauty
of the absent girl." The relationship has not
escaped Bagg (pp. 61-62) who notes that "the moon
is both a mental image of comparison and a sight
to behold; and the longed-for girl's essence
flows easily from the one into the other. . . .
Her beauty and far-off-ness and presence are
implicitly emanating from the moon. . . . Their
friend's personality is spreading toward them
through the medium of moonlight, encourages the
dew to make flowers blossom and will have a
reviving effect upon Atthis."

The papyrus contains eighteen additional
highly fragmentary verses. Of these only several
yield any sense: "For us, it is not easy to rival
goddesses in beauty of form, but you (?) . . ."
(21-23), and ". . . Aphrodite poured nectar from
a golden [bowl] . . ." (26-28).

§ 9 (49LP) The first line is quoted by Hephais-
tion, the second line by Plutarch. Terentianus
Maurus suggests by his version that the verses
were consecutive, though as Campbell suggests (p.
276), "one would never have guessed as much."
Sappho seems to be saying either that she loved
the girl before the girl merited such affection,
or that the girl's awkward exterior did not veil
her inner qualities or their potential.

2. *with little to show*: lit., "graceless, immature."
It is for the sake of this word (Gr., *acharis*)
that Plutarch quotes the verse. Calame (I, p.
401) notes that ancient sources understood the
Greek word to mean "at an age too young for mar-

riage": "The outward quality of grace thus becomes the mark of marriageability. In being a member of Sappho's circle, the young girl acquires not only the grace which makes her a beautiful woman, but the acquisition of this quality opens the door to marriage." See p. 40, above.

§ 10 (131LP) Quoted by Hephaistion together with the preceding and, as Lobel and Page suggest (pp. 92-93), perhaps to be taken with it. Maximus of Tyre tells us that as Prodicus and others were rivals to Socrates, so were Gorgo and Andromeda to Sappho. (For the relationship between Sappho and Socrates, see introduction, p. 31.) Andromeda did not, however, always win out. In a verse also quoted by Hephaistion, "Andromeda has her just deserts." Of Gorgo (an easy target as her name is Greek for *Gorgon*; see Lobel and Page, p. 134) we learn from scattered allusions that one Archeanassa "will be called the wife of Gorgo" and that certain people are "fully sated with Gorgo." Calame (I, p. 371) speaks of "Gorgo's circle" and the possibility of its sexual activities.

§ 11 (57LP) Quoted by Athenaeus (1.21b-c) apropos of Andromeda. The social standing of the girl in question would be much the opposite of the girl who spurns Anacreon in § 48.

§ 12 (137LP) The quotation is introduced by Aristotle (*Rhetoric* 1367a), as follows: "They reproach what is shameful in what they speak, do, and intend, as even Sappho composed when Alcaeus said, 'there's something I'd tell you *etc.*'" On the nature and circumstances of the exchange as quoted by Aristotle, see Bowra, pp. 224-227, and Page, pp. 106-109. Page observes that Sappho and Alcaeus certainly lived part of their lives in the same city, during the same time, and probably within the same aristocratic circle, but that we have not evidence about the nature or degree of their acquaintance. Marcus Holland, in his *Sappho: A Drama in Verse*, depicts a fully adversative relationship between the two.

4. *and weren't stirring your tongue in some scurrilous brew*: lit., "and your tongue were not concocting something base to say." The Greek phrase is both colorful and colloquial, *ekyka kakon* "concocting, stirring evil." Commentators have

116

been overly concerned over what is probably a mock-abusive tone: "Her [Sappho's] words are certainly chilly, if not harsh and disapproving, and the metaphor in *ekyka*, . . . is more colloquial than we should expect from her in such company" (Bowra, p. 225). ". . . an unusual metaphor, and more forcible than the context requires; but not necessarily offensive or ill-humored" (Page, p. 105).

§ 13 (15bLP)   Preserved on papyrus; nothing can be made of the first eight lines. The precise identity of Doricha is subject to queston (see Campbell, p. 268). Athenaeus (13.596b-c) says she was reviled by Sappho. The fragment's interpretation suffers from an inability to determine who the subjects of the main verse are. I understand the situation as follows. An unspecified suitor has suffered Doricha's rebuff; Doricha then has a change of heart. Sappho hopes Doricha will be denied the satisfaction of the suitor's renewed interest.

§ 14 (22LP)   Preserved on papyrus as vs. 11-14 of a nineteen verse fragment.

§ 15 (21bLP)   Quoted by Athenaeus (15.674e). Two unsuccessfully emended verses follow which appear to indicate the Graces' preference for what is garlanded.

§ 16 (23LP)   Preserved on papyrus as vs. 3-6 of a twelve verse fragment, following Page's (p. 138) restoration of the Greek text.

§ 17 (105aLP)   Quoted by Syrianus in his commentary on Hermogenes. Himerius says that Sappho compared the bride to an apple, the groom to Achilles. The fragment, then, formed part of an epithalamium. Gerber (p. 177) suggests that "just as the apple high up in the tree avoids being picked, so the girl avoids marriage until the proper time." On the other hand, "because the girl who values her position is hard to win she may be left hanging for want of a worthy man to pick her" (Stigers 1977, p. 91). The fragment may also connote a hint of "sour grapes." The rarest beauty is often most inaccessible. Failure to obtain it can result in pretended disconcern. For the erotic symbolism of apples, see § 3.1-8.

§ 18 (105cLP)   Quoted by Demetrius but without specific ascription of authorship. The resemblance to the preceding poem suggests that the lines may have formed part of an epithalamium. Stigers (1977, p. 91) notes the contrast in §§ 17 and 18 between "flower and vulnerability on the one hand and fruit and inaccessibility on the other. These are two modes of coming into a relationship with men." Catullus appears indebted to the image in Poem 62.39-47:

As a flower grows, hidden in a walled-off plot,
undetected by herds, uprooted by no plow,
which breezes nurture, sun and showers train
--many the boys, many the girls desiring it--
which whithers when shorn by the slender blade
--and none the boys, none the girls desiring it--
so a maiden prized remains while yet untouched.
When, once defiled, she's lost her flower
boys no longer find her lovely; girls, no longer
  dear.

See E. S. Stigers, "Retreat from the Male: Catullus 62 and Sappho's Erotic Flowers," *Ramus*, Vol. 6 (1977), pp. 83-102.

§ 19 (114LP)   Quoted by Demetrius. Two verses in the Greek, the second rather uncertain.

§ 20 (107LP)   Quoted by Apollonius Dyscolus.

§ 21 (104aLP)   Quoted by Demetrius who says that the charm of the verses lies in the repetition of the word, "(you) bring." As in the case of § 18, Catullus appears to have these verses in mind in his Poem 62.20-25:

Hesperus, what crueler star traverses heaven?
You tear a daughter from her mother's arms,
You tear her clinging from her mother's arms,
grant her maiden's grace to an ardent youth.
What crueler does the foe in laying cities waste?

As Sappho's verses are sometimes considered part of a wedding song, her continuation might have been, according to Campbell (p. 282), either "but evening does not bring the bride back to her parents' home" or "so evening brings the bride to her husband's home." I have taken the liberty of supplying a couplet in the spirit of the former suggestion.

1. *Hesperus*: *Esperos* in Sappho's unaspirated Aeolic and understood by the ancients as deriving from *es* or *eis* (into) + *pher* (bring), i.e., the Evening Star marks an in-gathering, and the couplet, as J. S. Clay, "Sappho's Hesperus and Hesiod's Dawn," *Philologus*, Vol. 104 (1980), pp. 302-305, explains, develops in accordance with this etymology: the Greek *pher-eis* (you bring) reverses *Es-per*(-os) in the name of the Evening Star. And the poem, as a whole, is intended as a counterpart to Hesiod's description (*WD* 578-581) of centrifugal dawn.

§ 22 (141LP)   Quoted by Athenaeus (10.425d).

§ 23 (105bLP)   Quoted by Hephaistion; author's name not given. Subjecting the groom to multiple comparisons seems to have been a "well known parlour game"; see Campbell, p. 284. The most eligible bachelor and maiden in Homer are compared to saplings; Achilles at *Il.* 18.56 and Nausicaa at *Od.* 6.163.

§ 24 (30LP)   Preserved on the same papyrus as § 4. My continuous rendering of the text follows Bowra's (p. 221) restoration.

4. *violet-girt*: Gr., *iokolpos*; *kolpos* "bosom, fold, garment."

9. *nightingale*: Known for its proverbial insomnia.

§ 25 (112LP)   Quoted by Hephaistion.

6. *You are graced with the Cyprian's honors*: The first half of the Greek verse is missing, lit., ". . . Aphrodite has honored you surpassingly." For "the Cyprian" = Aphrodite, see §§ 3.1, note; 94.2.

§ 26 (44LP)   Preserved on papyrus. The poem differs from most of Sappho's remaining poetry in being narrative, instead of highly personal, and in exhibiting, throughout, the characteristics of Epic dialect, meter and style. Such features are best explained by the poem's Epic theme. Though Homer nowhere depicts the marriage of Hector and Andromache, Sappho's treatment might have had its point of origin in a reference to Andromache's home (*Il.* 6.394-395). Homer's silence about the

119

version "must be Sappho's own invention" (so Bowra, p. 231). The theme, a well known part of the Epic tradition, is one to which Sappho brings her own distinctive emphases and flavor. Some of these are bitterly ironic. G. Nagy, *Comparative Studies in Greek and Indic Meter* (Cambridge, Mass.: Harvard U. Press 1974), pp. 137-139, notes (among other such features) that Sappho uses an epithet ("god-like," see note to v. 14, below) reserved in the *Iliad* for Achilles, Hector's killer, as an epithet for Hector and Andromache. To this line of thought I would add the more general similarity that the wedding couple's entrance (in a cart accompanied by shouts) bears to the entrance of Hector's ransomed corpse in the last book of the *Iliad*. Sappho's wedding poem comes close to being a funeral dirge in disguise. For a similar instance of a theme developed contrary to audience expectation, see § 5, notes.

1. The verse in translation condenses three fragmentary verses of Greek. A gap of one verse follows before v. 2. *Idaeus*: the chief herald of Troy.

2. *imperishable fame*: Gr., *kleos aphthiton*, a central concern of the Epic tradition and of Epic heroes, alike. For discussion, see J. Redfield, *Nature and Culture in the Iliad: The Tragedy of Hector* (Chicago: U. of Chicago Press 1975), pp. 31-39, and the more technical treatment by Nagy, *ibid.*, pp. 27-149.

5. *exquisite*: Gr., *abran*; see § 3.14.

6.- *bringing purple robes . . . untold*: Particularly
7. illustrative of Bowra's feeling (p. 231) that the poem's "appeal is not so much dramatic as pictorial."

8. *His father*: Hector's father, Priam, king of Troy.

10. *carriages*: Gr., *satinai*, a rare word which designates women's conveyance, as opposed to *arma* "chariot" (as in v. 13, "carts").

14. *like to the gods*: Gr., *ikeloi theois*, the term appears inverted (*theoeikelois*) as the final word in the poem (n. 26). See also § 2.15-16, notes.

17. [and lyre]: Supplied by Campbell in his printing of the Greek text; suggested as a possibility by Gerber.

18. *castanets*: Of all items mentioned (see esp. vs. 6-7), castanets alone appear nowhere in Homer.

19. *the wondrous echo reaches the skies*: Reminiscent of a stanza by Alcaeus (on the beauty contests in Lesbos):

> Where yearly the girls range about
> making show
> of their beauty in trailing gowns;
> where the sacred shout
> and its *wondrous echo*
> from the women about them *resounds*.

23. *mingled frankincense, cassia, and myrrh*: Sappho is the earliest writer to mention these. See also § 3.4.

25. *Paon*: A Homeric epithet for Apollo. The Paean seems originally to have been a hymn addressed to Apollo in his role as Healer (see Campbell, p. xix).

§ 27 (132LP) Quoted by Hephaistion. A papyrus line reads "She [Sappho] had a daughter Cleis named after her mother." The poem is three lines in Greek, the last of which requires a verb such as "I would not take." The rhythm of the words *chrysioisin anthemoisin* "golden flowers" is especially appropriate with its girlish lilt. Homer achieves a similar effect in the name of the Phaeacian princess, Nausicaa, with its repeated final vowel.

2. *precious Cleis*: Gr., *Kleis agapata*. J. Hallett, "Beloved Cleis," *Quaderni Urbinati di Cultura Classica*, Vol. 39 (1982), pp. 21-31, sees in *agapata* "a word for someone prized in a non-sexual way, specifically a parent's, or sole guardian's, sole offspring." Moreover, "for the first time on Greek literary record, we find an adjective previously used only for male only children, . . . applied to a daughter."

§ 28 (98LP) Preserved in fragmentary form on a papyrus written in the 3rd century B.C. and assumed by Page (p. 98) to be "by far the oldest extant papyrus of Sappho or Alcaeus." Sappho discusses a subject suitable to a young girl (most likely her daughter, Cleis; see § 27) -- the type of headband she should wear. If an expensive headband is unavailable, flowers will suit Cleis equally well. From the yet more fragmentary lines that follow, it seems that harsh circumstances during Sappho's exile have placed an item of such finery beyond her means. The following is decipherable from about ten verses: "Lately . . . a decorated headband from Sardis . . . for you, Cleis, I have no headband, and know not where I shall get one." Sappho then makes several political allusions (unusual in her poetry) and a mention of exile.

§ 29 (110LP)   Quoted by Hephaistion. The banter is similar to that of the following selection. At issue in both cases is exaggerated size. Commentators refer to the traditional attempted "rescue" of the bride by her friends after the couple had entered the bridal chamber. A friend of the groom who "protected" the chamber entrance is here the butt of Sappho's ridicule. *Risqué* abuse was a common feature of Greek wedding songs.

§ 30 (111LP)   Quoted by Demetrius. Bowra (p. 216), seeming somewhat embarrassed, limits his remarks to: "this is neither bawdy nor exalted, but playful. If the humor is a bit primitive, that is due to tradition, which expected jokes at this level." Campbell (p. 284) notes Kirk's suspicion of "indecency" in the final verse, but backs off by suggesting that "the fun may be childish," as in the preceding piece. Gerber (p. 179) is fuller in his endorsement: "If Kirk is right in his explanation that the bridegroom is so described 'because he is fantastically ithyphallic' (hence the order to raise the roof), this is the only example in Sappho of the ritual obscenity common in wedding-songs." The piece's style is in keeping with its meaning. Notes Demetrius: "The style in which she [Sappho] mocks the awkward bridegroom or the keeper of the wedding door is very different. It is quite commonplace, and the words are better suited to prose than to poetry. Indeed, these poems of hers can be better spoken than sung, and would not be suitable for the chorus or the lyre, unless for a kind of talking chorus."

2. *sing joy to the groom*: lit., "Hail Hymen" (the god of marriage), a one-word exclamation in Greek (*ymenaon*), and traditional for the wedding ceremony.

4. *give him more room*: The idea is but implicit in the original.

5. *equalling Ares he enters the door*: Perhaps a touch of the mock-heroic meant to recall *Il.* 11.604 where the phrase "he came forth equal to Ares" describes Patroclus as he enters the battle, clad in Achilles' armor, and soon to die as his surrogate. The precise reading of the verb ("enters") is uncertain in the preserved version of Sappho's text. Gerber (p. 179) does well in following Kirk's: "I take the adverbial 'like Ares' quite regularly as qualifying the action of the verb: 'will rush along' as Ares rushes into battle, emphasizing the bridegroom's impetuosity."

6. *more duly endowed than you built it for*: lit., "much bigger than a big man." Demetrius quoted the poem for the way in which this final verse gracefully modified the hyperbole of the one preceding.

§ 31 (51LP)   Quoted by Chrysippus.

§ 32 (50LP)   Quoted by Galen.

§ 33 (126LP)   Quoted in the *Etymologicum Genuinum* and *Etymologicum Magnum*.

§ 34 (102LP)   Quoted by Hephaistion. For the origin of the verses in popular tradition or folksong, see Gerber, p. 177.

§ 35 (47LP)   Lobel's generally accepted reconstruction of the paraphrase found in Maximus of Tyre: "Love racked her [Sappho's] heart, as a wind falling on oaks throughout the mountain." The violence of love, though here compared to wind (also § 91), is akin to that in the following fragment.

§ 36 (130LP)   Quoted by Hephaistion. Notes Bowra (p. 184): "In a very few words Sappho conveys the turmoil of her state which is both physical and mental and which she both welcomes and hates" (so also §§ 47, 73).

1. *again*: see § 1.5, note.

2. *dissolver of limbs*: Gr., *lysimeles*, a traditional epithet of love. See § 73, and *Th.* 120-122 for description of Eros, the primordial power (not "Cupid"): ". . . and [there was at first] Eros, the loveliest among the deathless gods, who *dissolves the limbs* and overpowers the mind and wise counsels of all gods and all men within them." Sappho, however, gives the traditional term new force by combining it with what follows; see further Bowra, p. 184.

3. *bittersweet*: Gr., *glykypikron*, an original compound in Sappho ("bitter and sweet" in other authors) not occurring again until Hellenistic times. Snell (p. 60) notes the daring freshness of the paradox first conveyed by the term, a paradox akin to that of §§ 46, 47; see note 46, above.

4. *irresistible*: Gr., *amachanon* "not to be devised against."

5. *creeping in*: Gr., *orpeton* "a crawler" (Eng., "serpent"), a neuter noun modified by the two preceding adjectives. The word, as Bowra notes (p. 184), is intentionally vague and can designate almost anything that moves on all four or creeps. It is for this reason that Eros is *amachanon*. (Hallett, p. 462, translates "surreptitious.")

§ 37 (48LP)   Quoted by Julian; suspected to be Sappho's.

§ 38 (Fr. Adesp. 976P)   Quoted by Hephaistion with no ascription to Sappho. Sappho's authorship, formerly doubted on dialectical grounds, is now beyond question. See A. W. Gomme, "Interpretations of Some Poems of Alkaios and Sappho," *JHS* Vol. 77 (1957), pp. 265-266, and especially D. Clay, "Fragmentum Adespotum 976," *TAPA* Vol. 101 (1970), pp. 119-129. Clay gives a survey of the history of scholarship on the poem (not a fragment but, with § 1, one of the two surely complete poems surviving from Sappho's works). The moon (personified in the poem as *Selanna*),

124

explains Clay, "sinks into the seas to join [her mythic lover] Endymion, but midnight comes on, the season of love passes by, and the human woman and poet must sleep alone." According to one version of the myth, the Moon Goddess made the handsome Endymion fall into a deep and eternal sleep in order to embrace him secretly. See J. Boardman & E. LaRocca, p. 128; also A. Weigall, pp. 287-290, for development of the idea that "Endymion was the ideal youth, physically to be desired, and in slumber not to be feared."

A. E. Housman twice translated the poem (*More Poems* Xl):

The rainy Pleiads wester,
  Orion plunges prone,
The stroke of midnight ceases,
  And I lie down alone.

More elaborate was his first version (*More Poems* X):

The weeping Pleiads wester,
  And the moon is under seas;
From bourn to bourn of midnight
  Far sighs the rainy breeze;

It sighs from a lost country
  To a land I have never known;
The weeping Pleiads wester
  And I lie down alone.

2. *Pleiad(e)s*: The seven daughters of Atlas and the ocean-nymph Pleione. Zeus transformed them into a constellation by way of saving them from the advances of the giant slayer, Orion. Their pursuer was set beside them in the skies (as in Housman's second version).

3. *hour*: Gr., *ora*, used in Homer to indicate the proper time or season for a thing -- most commonly for sleep or bed, and understood by Clay as "the season of the night" in Sappho's poem. Significant in this connection is that the notably pale and wavering Pleiads "served the whole ancient world as heralds of seasonal change"; see A. P. Burnett, "The Race with the Pleiades," *CP* Vol. 59 (1964), pp. 30-31 (apropos of Alcman's *Partheneion*, App. III).

§ 39 (59D)   The Rhipaean mountains were legendary. They were said to be beyond Scythia in the North on the boundary of the fabulous Hyperboreans (a legendary race of Apollo worshipers among whom, according to Delphic legend, the god spends his winters). See further Bowra, pp. 26-27, for the genre concerning marvels, wonders, and strange beings at the world's end to which this fragment might have belonged. *Evening's breast*: as Rhipe was a place never visited by the sun.

§ 40 (3D)   Preserved on a papyrus which dates to the end of the 1st century B.C., and first published in 1957. The poem had at least 126 verses, some sixty of which preceded the present segment. Of the sixty only vs. 7 - 10 yield any sense: "(the song) will at once scatter sweet sleep from my eyes/and desire drives me to go to the contest/ where especially I will toss my golden hair." The singers concentrate on the praises of another girl, Astymeloisa, who may be leading the worship. The text again becomes very fragmentary. The sense of verses 76ff seems to be, "If she took me by the soft hand, I should at once become her suppliant." For detailed reconstruction and interpretation, see Lasserre, pp. 10-13. The content, style, dialect and meter of this fragment closely resemble the same aspects of Alcman's *Partheneion* (Appendix III). Comparison of the two pieces occupies the better part of Calame, Vol. II, with a summary of results, pp. 144-146.

62. *casting glances more melting*: see § 94.

63. *her sweetness serves no idle whim*: The reading is uncertain. Otherwise translated "not at random is she sweet" (Page), "not at all in vain is she sweet" (Bowra).

64. *Astymeloisa*: means "Concern of the Town."

65. *garland*: The Greek word indicates a garland of the variety used in the worship of Hera. The girls, led by Astymeloisa, appear then to be making an offering to Hera in her capacity as goddess of birth and protectress of children, over whom she watches until they wed. See further Bowra, p. 34.

57.- The first two verses describe the rapidity and
58. ease of Astymeloisa's movement. Such comparison
to a star is frequent in archaic Greek poetry.
The third verse appears to describe her supple
form and the downy softness of her skin as per-
ceived from close by. The context, however,
remains uncertain.

71. *the moist charm of Cinyras*: A circumlocution for
Cyprian perfume or hair-oil. Cinyras was a king
of Cyprus which was famous for its scents.

73.- *in the host/people's darling*: "People's darling"
74. is a punning reference to Astymeloisa's name.
Hallett (p. 463) suggests that Astymeloisa's
appearance in "male society" may have marked a
debut, if not a wedding. The lines seem, in any
event, to indicate the public nature of the occa-
sion. See further § 54.

§ 41 (101D)   Quoted by Athenaeus (13.600f).

§ 42 (36D)   Quoted by Hephaestion as proverbial.

1.- *It isn't Aphrodite/but Eros, wild*: The contrast
2. is between a waggish Eros and a more demure and
tranquil Aphrodite. Such depictions suggest "the
calm before a storm" and are far less frequent
than those of love's maddening and precipitous
onslaught.

4.- *Down over the flower tops/heading this way*: lit.,
5. "coming down over the topmost flowers of the
clover." Plato (*Symposium* 195e) speaks of Eros'
most gentle step: "He proceeds not upon land nor
upon summits -- these are in no way delicate --
but amid the softest of all things existing does
he both proceed and reside." So also Aphrodite's
delicate step at *Th.* 194-195: "There came forth
[from the sea] a lovely and revered goddess, and
grass grew up about her from beneath her tender
feet." Sara Teasdale poignantly conveys the same
idea in her long poem, *Sappho* (III, 42-46): "Ah,
Love, there is no fleeing from thy might,/No
lonely place where thou hast never trod,/No
desert thou hast left uncarpeted/With flowers
that spring beneath thy perfect feet."

§ 43 (94D)   Quoted by Antigonus of Carystus. Antig-
onus explains that when male halcyons grow old
and can no longer fly, they are borne on the

wings of the female birds. So Alcman, weak with age, can no longer join in the maidens' song and dance.

1.- *with honey tones and voices of desire*: Gr., *meli-*
2. *garyes, hiarophonoi*, each English phrase a compound adjective.

7. *blue as the sea*: Gr., *haliporphyros*, also a compound adjective which is used in the *Odyssey* of purple wool and robes. See also §§ 48.1, 60.1.

§ 44 (58D)   Quoted by Apollonius the Sophist to show that Alcman used the word *knodalon* "seamonster." The theme of the sleep of nature, while common in Greek literature, is rarely described in such detail. If, as commentators suggest, a contrast is being made between the peaceful sleep of nature and, e.g., the poet's feverish love, the piece may have developed similar to § 91. The visual quality of Alcman's description is elaborated by C. M. Dawson, "*Spoudaiogeloion*: Random Thoughts on Occasional Poems," *YCS* Vol. 19 (1966), p. 60: "We travel down from the mountain peaks, step by step, via the river beds to the foothill promontories and gulfs at the seacoast; the animal world is broken down and shown in detail, from a general picture to animals of the mountains, creatures of the lower slopes and of the sea, all beneath the birds of the air. It is a conducted tour, of whose progress one might almost draw a picture."

ANACREON

§ 45 (37G)   Quoted by Clement of Alexandria.

1. *Exquisite*: see §§ 3.14, 26.5.

3.- *who . . . day*: see *Th.* 120-124.
4.

§ 46 (25G)   Quoted by Hephaistion. This vivid description of love's assault derives from *Od.* 9.391-393: "As when a smith plunges an axe or an adz, hissing greatly, in cold water, and tempers it -- for just that is the strength of iron. . ." Campbell notes (p. 328) that Anacreon's simile is

more violent than such images as he uses else-
where (e.g., §§ 64, 65). But this is precisely
the point, as few images could better convey the
rigors to which Love subjects its victim. The
burning lover is first hammered into submission;
forced to yield will and substance beneath Love's
incessant pounding. But a revitalized and better
tempered material emerges from the lover's oblit-
erated former self when he is plunged, as if bap-
tismally, into freezing torrents. Bowra (p. 290)
is uncharacteristically beside the point in stat-
ing that "Love has struck Anacreon a nasty blow
and left him in trouble . . . Anacreon is not
killed [as an ox struck by a similar blow at *Od.*
3.442-450], but he sees himself as at least
stunned."

§ 47 (46G)   Quoted by Hephaistion. Compare Catullus'
Poem 85.

Odi et amo. quare id faciam fortasse requiris?
    nescio, sed fieri sentio et excrucior.

I love and I hate. Why I do this perhaps you'd
    inquire?
I know not, but feel it occur, tormented entire.

§ 48 (13G)   This complete poem is quoted by Athenae-
us (13.599c) apropos of the untenable view that
Sappho   and   Anacreon   were   contemporaries:
"Chamaeleon in his *Concerning Sappho* declares
that according to some Sappho was the subject of
Anacreon's verses "Again . . . agree." Athenaeus
then quotes, only to disclaim, a stanza sup-
posedly written by Sappho in reply.

1. *Again*: For the repeated assaults of love, see §§
    1.15; 18; 36.1; 46.1; 47.1; 48.1; 67.2. It is
    possible that Anacreon's repeated use of the word
    indicates (as is not the case with Sappho) a cer-
    tain lack of seriousness. In a similar vein, §
    65.

    ball: Eros is, in later literature, depicted as a
    ball player (see § 65, notes). The ball is at
    times associated with the lover's heart as it is
    associated with the apple. See Gerber pp. 229-230
    and § 3.3, note.

    purple . . . blond(2) . . . *gaily*(3): The three
    adjectives in consecutive verses strike a vivid

129

color contrast with the poet's grey, or white, hair in the final verse. The poet speaks elsewhere of his grey hair; see §§ 68-70.

2. *play*: Such play is here, as elsewhere, amorous; see § 60.2.

3. *with a gaily sandaled girl*: For the erotic significance of feet (fascination and fixation) in antiquity, see J. Glenn, "Ariadne's Daydream (Catullus 64.158-163)," *CJ* Vol. 76 (1981), pp. 113-116.

4. *But she's of Lesbian pedigree*: lit., "But she is from well-built Lesbos." The term "well-built" is used in Epic of fine, or impressive cities (its use here being mock-heroic). My rendering emphasizes the girl's cosmopolitan credentials.

7. *gapes*: The Greek *chaskei* (Eng., "chasm") shares a coarseness with its translation "gapes" and indicates eager anticipation and undivided interest. Only here does it appear in an amatory context.

   gapes that some other girl agree: lit., "gapes toward another" (in hopes of a response). "Another" is feminine singular and thus indicates, without the use of "girl" in Greek, the gender of the person in question (so also § 1.20). This is the only ancient text in which there is an express association between Lesbos and homosexuality. The poem has, alternatively, been seen as an expression of the girl's heterosexual selectivity. L. Woodbury, "Gold Hair and Grey, or The Game of Love: Anacreon Fr. 13G," *TAPA* Vol. 109 (1979), pp. 277-287, understands "gapes toward another" with reference to "another head of hair" and not to "another (feminine) person." Notes Woodbury (pp. 284-286): "The poem finds its point in a contrast between two heads of hair, of which one is spurned by the girl because of its whiteness, while the other is the object of open-mouthed desire. The hair [by synecdoche] signifies both the person and the object of love. . . . The girl [is] turning from one head to another in search for a suitable object of *Eros* . . . . The marked and unusual emphasis that Anacreon has given here to the head and its hair has been prepared for by his choice of the epithet *chrysokomos* [golden-haired]." Significant to this interpretation is the question posed by A. W. Gomme (§ 38, notes), p. 259, n. 13: "And why should Anakreon say that he was scorned for his white hair, if he was only scorned because he was a man?" See further Dover (p. 183) for other possibilities as to which and whose hair is at issue.

§ 49 (78G)   Quoted by Heraclitus together with examples from Archilochus and Alcaeus as an example of allegory: "Anacreon, abusing the meretricious spirit and arrogance of a haughty woman, used the allegory of a horse to describe her frisky disposition." Campbell (p. 328) notes that if Heraclitus has quoted the entire piece, we need not take such a solemn view of what has the air of a light-hearted poem, charming because of its imagery and its *risqué* metaphor.

Bowra (p. 272) speaks eloquently of the poem's place in Greek poetry and merits lengthy quotation: "This strikes a new note in Greek poetry; for it is both lyrical and witty, both passionate and fanciful . . . . The comparison of the girl with a filly recalls Alcman's treatment of Hagesichora and her friends [App. III], but the skill and precision with which the image is developed and completed shows that Anacreon has found his own individual voice. The wit comes in the amatory undertones . . . . He faces the facts, and smiles while he sings of his desire, and a note of sly mockery is audible among words which are perfectly apt and delicate . . . . Anacreon enjoys the situation and knows that others will enjoy it too. His head understands his heart, but refuses to make too many overt concessions to it."

1.   *Thracian filly*: Thracian horses were famous from Homer's time onward. For references in ancient literature, see Campbell, pp. 328-329; Gerber, pp. 236-237. Hesychius glosses "filly" as "courtesan."

5.   *you lightly skip*: lit., "lightly skipping you play." For the erotic connotations of "play," see § 48.2.

6.   *hug your hip*: lit., "mount you," with the same connotation in Greek as in English.

§ 50 (22G)   Quoted by Maximus of Tyre.

131

§ 51 (15G)   Quoted by Athenaeus (13.564d) to illustrate the attention given by lovers to the eyes of their beloved.

4.   *my soul's unwitting charioteer*: lit., "(you) not knowing that you *drive the chariot* of my soul" (italics a single word in Greek). Campbell notes (p. 322) that the metaphor is well placed as the last word of the stanza. See also § 94.

§ 52 (83G)   Quoted by a scholiast to Aristophanes' *Birds*. Anacreon proposes to remedy a young boy's rejection of his advances by appealing directly to Eros. Bowra (p. 305) suggests the lines might be part of a poem to which the preceding verses also belong. See further § 67.2, note.

§ 53 (96G)   Quoted several times by Athenaeus (14.634a, 635c) in discussion of the precise type of "lyre" designated by the rare Gr., *magis*.

§ 54 (60G)   Preserved on a papyrus. Four fragmentary stanzas in the Greek. Bowra (pp. 286-289) believes the addressee a boy; Gentili (pp. 45, 187-191), a girl. The opening vocative phrase "O most beautifully faced of children" leaves the gender in question as do the pronouns in vs. 4 and 8. The poem's extant verses, notes Bowra (p. 289), fall into three stages -- the boy's shy, restricted life at home, his discovery of Aphrodite, and his appearance in public. The first and last stages are presented realistically, and the second, by contrast, is placed in the world of myth. For the erotic significance of horses and meadows, see § 3.10.

5.- *but you . . . run*: Bowra notes (p. 288) that in
7.   introducing the field of hyacinth, Anacreon does yet more strikingly what he does in making Eros a youth with golden hair who throws a ball [§ 48]. He gives substance to a state of mind by making it entirely visual and concrete and enriching it with mythic associations. The meadow then is symbolic of desire's awakening; contrast § 90.3.

8.- *In the midst . . . town*: The Greek verb "dart"
9.   often appears in Homer to convey the rapidity of a god or goddess' movement, especially when the divinity proceeds from the heights of Olympus to Earth. The verb "flutter" is the same as appears

in § 14.3. The point of the third and first stanzas seems to be that the boy's heart beats quickly (i.e., is frightened) at the awe-filled or stupefied expressions that his beauty (without his realizing it) occasions in the onlooker. But when the boy darts through the streets, oblivious to those he passes, it is the townsfolk whose hearts race. See D. M. Robinson and E. Fluck, *A Study of the Greek Love-Names, Including a Discussion of Pederasty and a Prosopographia* (Baltimore: Johns Hopkins Press 1937), p. 3, for the idea that "the admiration for a beautiful youth must often have been city-wide and not merely the personal feeling of a single individual."

§ 55 (19G)   Quoted by Athenaeus (15.671d). Notes Bowra (p. 277): "So too he [Anacreon] takes pride in Megistes' part in the worship of Dionysus, whose cult . . . may have been the special concern of boys who had reached the age of puberty."

1. *the season comes round:* lit., "(it is) ten months since."

§ 56 (99G)   Quoted in *Etymologicum Magnum*.

1.- *I . . . quiet:* lit., "I hate all who have under-
4. ground and difficult manners. I have learned that you, O Megistes, are *of those who do not play the Bacchant.*" Gr. (for the italicized words), *ton abakidzomenon*. The *Et. Magn.* cites the verses for the occurrence of the word. The Bacchants were the frenzied followers of Dionysus (known also as Bacchus).

§ 57 (43G)   Quoted by the scholiast on Pindar's *Olympian Ode* 7 to illustrate the meaning of the verb *propino*: "extend, yield, surrender, bestow."

§ 58 (28G)   Quoted by Athenaeus (9.396d) and others apropos of whether the female (deer) has horns. Notes Bowra (p. 294): ". . . when he [Anacreon] makes the mother horned, it is perhaps to show that she is somehow formidable. The truth of the lines lies not in zoological precision but in the way they hit off the gentle shyness of a boy who is like a young fawn."

§ 59 (76G)   Quoted by a scholiast on Sophocles' *Antigone* in explanation of the verb. A single verse in Greek.

§ 60 (14G)   Quoted by Dio Chrysostom to illustrate the inappropriateness of a king's calling on a god in the manner of Anacreon.

1. *Master*: The divinity is Dionysus who is named in the last verse of the Greek.

    rosy: Gr., *porphyree* "purple" the same Greek word as in § 48.1. The appropriateness of the word to Aphrodite is variously explained. She is rosy "because of the glow that shines from her" (Bowra, p. 284); the adjective "is spoken in reference to the goddess or her garment which shines as a rainbow with different colors" (Gentili, p. 13 [notes], following a late 19th century Latin dissertation on Anacreon). Gerber (p. 228) suggests "radiant" or "dazzling." The Greek word is frequent in descriptions of the sea and has accordingly occasioned interpretation deriving from Aphrodite's birth in the sea. See further §§ 1.7, 42.4-5. Bowra does well to note (p. 283) that "He [Anacreon] imagines the god with his joyous company and . . . makes them vivid not by the stock epithets derived from epic but by new epithets of his own minting." For the association of Aphrodite and Dionysus, see Euripides, *Bacchae* 402-416, and E. R. Dodds' note *ad. loc.* in his edition of the play. The Nymphs were Dionysus' nurses.

2. *play*: See § 48.2, note.

7. *Cleobulus be well advised*: lit., "be a good counsellor [Gr., *symboulos*] to kleo*boulos*." The play on words suggests a light tone (contrast § 1) as Anacreon implores Dionysus' help in winning over Cleobulus, i.e., that a drunken Cleobulus yield to the poet's advances.

§ 61 (5G)   Quoted by Herodian to illustrate the figure called *polyptoton* (lit., "much falling"), the repetition of a word in different grammatical cases (as in Tennyson's [*Maud* I, 672] "my own heart's heart, my ownest own, farewell"). Gerber (p. 229) takes the figure to indicate that the poet, as elsewhere, is only partly serious.

3. *I gaze*: Gr., *dioskeo*, a rare verb, explained by Hesychius: "*to gaze*: to look continuously, not altering one's glance. [The word] is used of being swept away in body and soul."

§ 62 (33G) Quoted by Athenaeus (10.427a) to illustrate the proportion for mixing wine and water. The mixture here is weak by any standard (Alcaeus calls for 1:2, a blend four times as potent) and indicates the poet's sense of decorum even when he would revel. The symposium, despite its moderated drinking, appears to have gotten out of hand in the last four verses.

§ 63 (56G) Quoted by Athenaeus (11.463a) for the correct conduct at a symposium. The translation expands somewhat on the four verses of the original.

§ 64 (38, 65G) Quoted by Athenaeus (11.782a) as evidence that the ancients, when mixing wine, poured the water into the bowl before the wine. Demetrius noted that the poem's rhythm was precisely that of a drunk old man. As both are remote concerns for readers today, attention should focus on the imagistic playfulness of "going a round" with Eros. The image is highlighted by Anacreon's use of the Greek verb *pyktalizo* (found only here) in place of the usual *pykteuo* "to box." The same image is used with greater power and solemnity by Sophocles in his *Women of Trachis* (441-442): "Whoever stands up to Eros for a round of fisticuffs, has lost his wits." See further Bowra, p. 293. That Anacreon did not always leave the ring unscathed is evident from a rejoinder (*I who sparred . . .*) preserved on papyrus (65.1-2G).

§ 65 (111G) Quoted from Anacreon by a scholiast on *Il.* 23.88 where the same word "dice" occurs. Eros and the equally young and attractive Ganymede (seized by Zeus to be his "cupbearer") are depicted at play with dice, or knucklebones, by Apollonius Rhodius (3.117ff) and by one Asclepiades in a poem (12.46) preserved in the *Palatine Anthology* (see T. M. Klein, "Eros' Golden Ball," *CW* Vol. 74 [1981] pp. 225-227). The last word of the poem is *kydoimoi*, an Epic word meaning "din of battle, uproar." The elevated diction adds a mock-heroic tone. This touch, notes Campbell (p. 327), combined with the frivolous imagery of the dice and the playful meter, shows how little Anacreon took love's anguish seriously.

§ 66 (108G) Quoted by Athenaeus (10.433ef). Spoken to a woman ("generous" feminine in the Greek).

§ 67 (94G)   Quoted by Hephaistion. See pp. 32-36, above, for discussion.

1. *Drunk with love*: Bowra (p. 290) suggests that, since Euripides' Cyclops also jumps drunk from the Leucadian cliff (*Cyclops* 166-167), "those who made the leap sometimes comforted or steeled themselves first with drink, and Anacreon may have made use of the idea for his own purpose."

2. *Leucadian Rock*: see n. 58, above. To leap from the high rock on the island's southern tip was "to cure unrequited love or win the heart of a recalcitrant lover" (Gerber, p. 232). See G. Nagy (p. 146) for the "sexual element inherent in the motif of a white rock" and for the latent motif of sexual relief through jumping. As plunging is symbolic of sexual relief, Nagy notes the opposite in § 52 as symbolic of sexual frustration.

§ 68 (84G)   Bergk's (see Appendix I) restoration of a prose statement quoted in Lucian. For such reconstruction see also §§ 35, 87.

§ 69 (74G)   Quoted by Hephaistion. Gentili (p. 55) cites scholarship suggesting that the addressee might be a goddess. The epithet "gowned in gold" is used by other Greek authors of goddesses.

§ 70 (36G) Quoted by Stobaeus. The only poem by Anacreon serious enough to find a place in his anthology.

10.- *and hard . . . infinite*: lit., "and hard is the
12. descent into it [Hades], for it is certain that the one who has gone down will not come up." Commentators, while noting the idea is a commonplace, do not give Virgil's adaptation its due (*Aeneid* 6.126-129):

> . . . *facilis descensus Averno*:
> noctes atque dies patet atri ianua Ditis;
> sed revocare gradum superasque evadere ad auras
> hoc opus, hic labor est.

> . . . *easy is the descent to Hell*:
> night and day the gates of dreary Dis lie open;
> but to recall one's step, proceed to open air,
> this is the task, here the travail.

§ 71 (203T)   Quoted by Stobaeus.

§ 72 (197T)   Quoted by Stobaeus.

2. *eyes beset with thickest mist*: The "misting" of one's eyes is a frequent element in Homeric descriptions of death. Compare § 2.11.

§ 73 (212T)   Quoted by Hephaistion. Compare § 36.

§ 74 (111T)   Quoted by Plutarch apropos of the formulation used in beginning a prayer ("If only I might . . ."). The interpretation of a lover's wish puts the poet's feeling toward Neoboule at a variance with that in the following section. The statement might, alternatively, be an expression of the rejected poet's animus: "Might my hand but lay hold of Neoboule"! As such, the statement suggests according to Kirkwood (p. 41), "violent revenge or even a savage violation, akin to the coarse and vigorous lines in [§ 88], in the same meter."

§ 75 (196aW)   The near decade since the poem's discovery (1973) has witnessed a vast outpouring of scholarly discussion on matters of authorship (firm attribution to Archilochus), textual reconstruction (papyrus obliterated to left and right) and interpretation (dependent on reconstruction and for that reason, among others, expectedly at great variance). The pioneering work in English has been by John Van Sickle. See:

1. "The New Erotic Fragment of Archilochus," *Quaderni Urbinati di Cultura Classica*, Vol. 20 (1975), pp. 123-156.

2. "Archilochus: A New Fragment of an Epode," *Classical Journal*, Vol. 71 (1975), pp. 1-15 (includes a verse translation into English).

3. "The Doctored Text/Translating a New Fragment of Archilochus," *Modern Language Notes*, Vol. 90 (1975), pp. 872-885 (includes discussion of five translations into English, largely of the poem's conclusion).

4. **The New Archilochus**, *Arethusa*, Vol. 9, No. 2, 1976 (J. Van Sickle, ed.). Contains the following:

J. Van Sickle, "The New Archilochus Texts," "Introduction," "Select Bibliography for the Cologne Epode," pp. 129-150.

D. Campbell, "The Language of the New Archilochus," pp. 151-158.

J. Henderson, "The Cologne Epode and the Conventions of Early Greek Erotic Poetry," pp. 159-179.

M. Lefkowitz, "Fictions in Literary Biography: the New Poem and the Archilochus Legend," pp. 181-189.

G. Nagy, "Iambos: Typologies of Invective and Praise," pp. 191-205.

L. E. Rossi, "Asynarteta from the Archaic to the Alexandrian Poets: On the Authenticity of the New Archilochus," pp. 207-229 (highly technical piece on the poem's original meter).

As the poem opens (following the loss of an undeterminable number of lines), a young girl urges restraint in the face of a would-be lover's advances. Her reluctance seems prompted by the fact that the proposed "sex here and now" includes no plan of marriage. She thus urges his affections on Neoboule, perhaps her older sister (line 22), as one more suited to his designs. "What the girl must be saying, albeit indirectly, is that she herself is willing to be seduced if her seducer promises marriage first. By mentioning another maiden the girl obliquely offers herself under what she considers the best obtainable conditions" (Henderson, pp. 168-169).

The alternative girl is expectedly unacceptable. The man in dignified terms invokes the young girl's departed mother, as if to suggest that the mother's high ideals ("no sex without marriage") are buried with her. The girl must decide things for herself. In the most enigmatic phrase of the poem (line 13), the man offers a compromise in the form of "a joy aside from [or, *just outside of*] the divine" -- apparently some

138

kind of activity which will allow sexual release
for him without violating her, an activity
brought to completion in the closing lines (see
further Van Sickle, *CJ* pp. 9-30; *MLN* pp. 879,
881).

Alternatively (see Henderson, p. 171),
"aside from the divine" (13) = marriage; "as you
urge so shall I go" (17) = will marry you; "I'll
put in where the grass is lush" (21) = deflora-
tion (as indicated by "released all my force and
fell tame" [47] -- though the speaker "delicately
avoids mentioning the actual penetration"); "just
touching [on] the tawny hair" (48) -- i.e., hair
of the head.

The poem's interpretation has greatly bene-
fited from comparison and contrast with famous
scenes of seduction or potential seduction in
Homer, specifically, Hera's seduction of Zeus
(*Iliad* 14) and Odysseus' meeting of Nausicaa
(*Odyssey* 6); see Van Sickle *CJ*, pp. 10-13 and
QUCC, pp. 123-156.

Though our translations are at great stylis-
tic variance, I am indebted to Van Sickle's (*CJ*,
pp. 1-2) for my opening and closing lines and for
the use of "reconnoitered" in line 47. Notes Van
Sickle (*MLN*, p. 878): "erotic action generalized
to the whole body after the provocative view
above. A magnificent verb from epic vocabulary,
amphaphomenos, full and drawn out in the deliber-
ate iambic rhythm, suggests the process of dis-
covery, fondling, running over, exploring --
'reconnoitering.'"

§ 76 (109T)   Quoted by Athenaeus (10.433e). Compare
§ 66.

§ 77 (190T)   Quoted by Plutarch.

1. *Such did she conspire*: lit., "devising deceit-
   fully" (she bore in one hand etc.).

§ 78 (1T)   Quoted by Athenaeus (14.627c) as evidence
of the poet's equal emphasis on civic and poetic
activities. D. Page (*Fondation Hardt*, p. 134)
notes the novelty of the theme: "In the Epic, a
man may be as good in speech as in action (*Il.*
9.443), and a great warrior might pass the time
singing a song (*Il.* 9.189), but it is inconceiv-

able that the same man could be both soldier and poet. . . . A social revolution is epitomised in this couplet . . ." Notes Kirkwood (p. 31): "By pairing the two traditionally separate activities, Archilochus is asserting a new role in society, characteristic of the century that followed him and played both by the elegist-politician Solon and by the lyricist-politician Alcaeus [see n. 32, above] -- a role that makes the man of the Muses no longer the onlooker."

1. *Enyalius*: As in Homer, synonymous with Ares.

§ 79 (2T)   Quoted by Athenaeus (1.30f). A good soldier's vigilance knows no unpreparedness. The couplet has occasioned numerous interpretations, all depending on the meaning of the thrice repeated Gr., *en dori*, lit., "in my spear"; e.g., "equipped with my spear," "in or on a tree," "in my ship." (The Greek word's basic meaning is "stem of a tree," hence "plank" and "ship.") According to the interpretation based on "in my spear" ("In my spear is my bread, in my spear is my wine" etc.), the poet depends on his weapon for the basics of existence. This is unlikely not so much, as commentators suggest, for grammatical reasons, as for the lack of parallel to wine and bread as the stated objectives of a soldier's fighting. Soldiers fight for *fame* (Gr., *kleos*; see § 26.2, note). And while they cannot be expected to fight on an empty stomach (*Il.* 19.154-174), the provenance of their "daily bread" goes unemphasized. Be that as it may, it appears that Archilochus did not intend the Greek "*en dori*" to be understood identically in all three instances. The desire to play with the phrase may, in fact, have motivated the couplet. This, and the poem's various interpretations, are discussed by N. Rubin, "Radical Semantic Shifts in Archilochus," *CJ* Vol. 77 (1981), pp. 6-7, who favors the idea of the poet's dependence on his spear for bread and wine.

§ 80 (96T)   Quoted by Dio Chrysostom. The poet will have no part of a foppish or affected commander. Four verses in the Greek.

3. *who most about his beard does fret*: Gr., *hypexy-remenon*, lit., "shaven out from under" or "partly shaven." A styled beard would require more to-do than one grown for the sake of not shaving.

4. *whose hairdo is his pride*: lit., "proud over his locks."

5. *spare and smart*: lit., "small and knock-kneed." Notes Gerber (p. 27), "it is courage, not size or physical appearance which counts."

§ 81 (105T)   Quoted by Stobaeus. One of the more expansive examples of self-exhortation in archaic poetry. See e.g., *Il.* 22.98; *Od.* 5.407, 20.18. From line 2 ("bearing your chest") onward, the poet, as N. Rubin observes (pp. 1-6, see § 79, notes), transforms his heart (Gr., *thymos*) from the seat of emotion to the individual winner or loser having that emotion. Moreover, *thymos* in Homer refers either to the emotions, the will or intellect. "Here, however, the meanings implied by *thymos* shift three times -- from heart (as seat of emotions) to spirit or courage to heart again and finally to mind or soul (as seat of thought)."

§ 82 (8T)   Compiled from quotations in several authors, referred to and imitated by many others. Notes Gerber (p. 15), "the flippant attitude toward warfare revealed in this famous fragment stands in stark contrast to the epic and the Spartan concept of valor which demanded that a warrior return from battle either with his shield or on it."

3. *Let it go to Hell*: Quite literally the meaning of Gr., *erreto*.

4. *another will serve me no less well*: lit., "I will again purchase one not worse."

§ 83 (102T)   Quoted by Stobaeus. As in the preceding piece, the poet is at the ready to debunk a popular notion: that fame and glory are undying and worth dying for. See § 26.2.

§ 84 (16T)   Quoted by Athenaeus (13.594d). Figs and fishing were the mainstays of poverty-stricken Paros. So fragment 87T: "Good riddance to Paros, and those figs, and the life of the sea." The fig was known for its cheapness, while designating, in Aristophanes, *Peace* 1350, *pudenda muliebria*.

2. *accessible, loved by all, to all exposed*: lit., "Pasiphile [= dear to all], good-natured, recep-

tive to strangers." Pasiphile is the last word of the couplet and subject of the comparison. Notes Gerber (p. 18): "An effective polarity is . . . obtained between the first and last words. The couplet begins with an apparently innocuous and unambiguous expression, but when we come to the second verse and view the poem as a whole we see that the first verse is a metaphor and the imagery is erotic and satirical."

§ 85 (44T)   Quoted by a scholiast on Aratus.

§ 86 (43T)   Quoted in the *Etymologicum Magnum*.

§ 87 (118T)   Second verse quoted by Aelian. The first verse is a possible reconstruction by F. Lasserre (1950 edition of Archilochus) deduced from a prose paraphrase in Nicetas of the whole. For such "reconstruction" see §§ 35, 68.

§ 88 (112T)   Quoted by a scholiast on Euripides' *Medea*. Sometimes thought to be the sequel to § 74 (both are in the same Greek meter). If so, a vivid illustration of the "tenderness and aggressive sensuality" which encompass the poet's erotic experience. "[The] harsh, raw side of Archilochus' poetic expression contrasts with his aptitude for generating impressions of his own sensibility." See Rankin (pp. 65-68) for these and other such formulations as point to Archilochus as "the first poet in the Greek world whom we know to have used deliberately this duality as a poetic motif."

1. *skin*: Gr., *askos* "wineskin."

    insatiable: Gr., *dresten* "hardworking." The phrase shows contempt and sexual ferocity. Kirkwood translates (p. 41) "slavish bag."

§ 89 (25, 26T)   The first two verses are quoted by Ammonius; the last three (two in the Greek), by Synesius, who says the poet is praising a courtesan's hair. The two fragments are often taken consecutively.

1.- *myrtle ... rose*: Symbols of Aphrodite which, ac-
2. cording to Rankin (p. 67), "would probably not be held so boldly by an entirely respectable maiden." See further J. S. Henderson, *The Maculate Muse* (New Haven: Yale U. Press 1975), p. 150.

142

§ 90 (27T)   Preserved on papyrus.

2.   *despair*: lit., "fall in love."

IBYCUS

§ 91 (6D)   Quoted by Athenaeus (13.601bc) as an example of Ibycus' love poetry. The poem strikes a contrast between "the seasonal regularity of nature and the ever present love of Ibycus which knows no season" (Campbell, p. 310). So also, the contrast between the serenity of Spring and the devastating onslaught of the poet's passion.

1.   *river streams bedew*: The rivers are led through the orchards in channels for irrigation.

2.   *quinces in Cydonia*: The quince trees of Cydonia (in northwest Crete) are related to the awakening of love. The lyric poet, Steisichorus (n. 48, above), writing of the wedding of Menelaus and Helen, describes the throwing of "many Cydonian 'apples'" (= quinces; see § 3.3, note). Ibycus intends the quince as a familiar symbol of love which swells to ripeness as girls grow to maidenhood. Grigson elaborates (p. 200): "In early Spring, the beginning of the special season of love, the five sepals of each quince flower bend back from a remarkably firm bud, which is pointed, and at first less pink than brown. The bud swells and stands erect, opening to its rose-like shape of tender pink, each petal lightly netted and veined."

3.   *sacred* (or *"inviolate"*) . . . *Maidens' grove*: The countryside nymphs are probably intended. Euripides has the virginal Hippolytus offer Artemis a garland of flowers in just such a place (*Hippolytus* 73-78). Such places symbolize unsoiled innocence; contrast § 54.5-6.

4.   *shaded bough vine-blossomed grows*: To the images of quinces and inviolate enclosures, Ibycus adds that of budding vines with their associations of youthful growth. He conveys the natural growth from innocence to love through the figure of grapes swelling to fullness. The first image (quinces) suggests the ripening of girlhood

143

toward love; the second (inviolate meadows), the secure innocence in which it lives; the third (vine blossoms), the moment before it is ready for marriage. For these and further observations, see Bowra, pp. 260-262.

5. *this love of mine no season knows*: lit., "my love is no time 'at rest' or 'at bed'" (Gr., *katakoitos*, only here).

6. *northern Thracian blast*: For love as a wind, see § 35. Ancient writers considered the Thracians a primitive people consisting mainly of ferocious mountain tribes.

9. *parching rage*: in contrast to v. 1, "river streams bedew."

10. *It racks my frame, unceasingly*: lit., "it violently strikes me from the feet (up)."

§ 94 (7D) Parmenides, in the Platonic dialogue bearing his name (137a), paraphrases these verses in expressing his reluctance to embark on a lengthy exposition. The scholiast provides the actual passage by Ibycus. The poem is most likely complete. The poet here feels himself past the age for love and trembles at the approaching prospect of being, once again, "harnessed." Yet he is no more capable of running love's course than he is of resisting the yoke. He will be forced to stumble through love's paces. That the theme is a commonplace with the lyric poets in no way detracts from Ibycus' unique expression of it. Compare §§ 43, 68-70, 90.

1. *Love's melting look*: lit., "eyeing (me) meltingly." Compare § 40.2.

   from eyes dark-browed: Compare Hesiod's description of the Graces (*Th.* 910-911): "Love flows from their gazing eyes, a limb-loosing love. And beguilingly they gaze from beneath their lids."

2.- *Cyprian chains*: The chains (lit., "nets") of
3. Aphrodite are inescapable. Her boy, Eros, seduces the prey into them.

5. *as a horse*: See §§ 3.10, 54.

V

GLOSSARY

The following list briefly identifies the
authors whose works preserve so much of
extant Greek lyric (all except what is pre-
served on papyri and, in one case, § 3, on
pottery). Citations are adapted from *The
Oxford Classical Dictionary*, N. G. L. Ham-
mond and J. J. Scullard, editors; Oxford
University Press, 1970².

Aelian (2nd and 3rd c. A.D.)   Pontifex at Praeneste,
   taught rhetoric at Rome, wrote works of a moraliz-
   ing nature.

Alexandrian Age (4th - 1st c. B.C.)   The period when
   Alexandria in Egypt, thanks to its library and mu-
   seum, was the literary capital of the Greek world.

Ammonius (2nd c. B.C.)   Pupil and successor of the
   great Alexandrian scholar, Aristarchus; grammarian
   and commentator on the works of Homer.

Antigonus of Carystus (3rd c. B.C.)   Athenian writer
   connected with Plato's Academy, author of anecdotal
   writings.

Apollonius Dyscolus (2nd c. A.D.)   Alexandrian gram-
   marian at Rome under the Emperor, Marcus Aurelius,
   known for his exactitude, obscurity of style, and
   asperity of manner (*dyskolos* = "harsh, severe").

Apollonius of Rhodes (3rd c. B.C.)   A leading figure
   of the Alexandrian Age (q.v.), author of the first
   fully extant account of Jason and the Argonauts.

Apollonius the Sophist (2nd c. A.D.)   Alexandrian
   Homeric scholar.

Aratus (4th and 3rd c. B.C.)   Best known for his
   major extant work, an astronomical poem entitled
   Phaenomena.

Athenaeus (2nd and 3rd c. A.D.)   Lived in Naucratis
   (Egypt). His only extant work is the *Deipnosophis-
   tai* (*Doctors at Dinner*) now in fifteen books

145

(though perhaps originally in thirty). At the ban-
quet which extends over several days, philosophy
law, literature, medicine, and other topics are
discussed by the authoritative guests. In the
course of this symposium, the author cites some
1,250 authors, gives the titles of more than 1,000
plays, and quotes more than 10,000 lines of verse.
Much of this information and material would other-
wise be lost to us. See bibliography.

Augustan Age (27 B.C. - 14 A.D.)   The golden age of
Roman culture under the reign of the emperor
Augustus.

Catullus (1st c. B.C.)   Roman love poet *par excel-
lence*, author of a small collection (*libellus*) in
praise (and despair of) his faithless mistress,
Lesbia. Other poems include wedding hymns, politi-
cal lampoons (against Julius Caesar) and a 400
verse epic on the Marriage of Peleus and Thetis.

Clement of Alexandria (2nd and 3rd c. A.D.)   Alexan-
drian churchman, author of extant works arguing the
merits of Christianity over pagan religions and
philosophies.

Chrysippus (3rd c. B.C.)   Life devoted to elaborating
the Stoic system in numerous works. His philosophy
became identified with Stoic orthodoxy.

Demetrius (4th and 3rd c. B.C.)   Author of a trea-
tise, *On Style*. The work, in the course of elabo-
rating upon the meager, florid, grand, and fearsome
classes of rhetoric, quotes poets, historians, ora-
tors and numerous minor 4th c. figures.

Dio Chrysostom (1st and 2nd c. A.D.)   called *Chrysos-
tomus* (*Golden-mouthed*) for his rhetorical prowess.
Author of some eighty speeches on a variety of
themes. Many of these are display-pieces extolling
Stoic ideals.

Diodorus (1st c. B.C.)   Author (in Greek) under
Julius Caesar and Augustus of a *World History*, in
forty books, from the earliest times to Caesar's
Gallic War (54 B.C.).

Dionysius of Halicarnassus (1st c. B.C.)   Rhetor and
historian, wrote in Greek and taught at Rome for
many years. His treatise *On Literary Composition* is
the only surviving ancient work on word arrangement

146

and euphony, and preserves our only surely complete Sapphic poem (§ 1).

Etymologicum Genuinum   A late 9th c. A.D. lexicon which, together with the *Etymologicum Gudianum* (circa A.D. 1100), served as the basis of the *Etymologicum Magnum*.

Etymologicum Magnum   An extant lexicon of uncertain date, but used by the great classical scholar and churchman Eustathius, who became Archbishop of Thessalonica in A.D. 1175.

Eustathius (12 c. A.D.)   Deacon at St. Sophia in Constantinople and commentator of classical works, the *Iliad* and *Odyssey*, in particular. See preceding reference.

Galen (2nd c. A.D.)   Court physician at Rome to the Emperor, Marcus Aurelius. Author of philosophical treatises and medical books.

Hellenistic Age (4th - 1st c. B.C.)   Period following the death of Alexander the Great (323 B.C.) which marked the spread of Greek culture throughout the known world. See also Alexandrian Age.

Hephaistion (2nd c. A.D.)   Greek metrist whose mammoth forty-eight volume treatise *On Meter* was reduced by successive abridgements to a single volume *Handbook* (or *Encheiridion* = "in the hand") in which form it is now extant.

Heraclitus (6th c. B.C.)   Presocratic philosopher who conceived the universe as a ceaseless conflict of opposites regulated by the unchanging law which he designated as *Logos*. His work survives in fragments only.

Hermogenes (2nd c. A.D.)   Greek writer admired by Marcus Aurelius. Author of *On Forms* which deals with seven qualities of style, all to be seen as ingredients in the perfection of the orator, Demosthenes.

Herodian (2nd c. A.D.)   Son of Apollonius Dyscolus (see above), wrote works on the accentuation of the *Iliad* and *Odyssey*. Ranks with his father as one of the greatest, as he is the last, of original Greek grammarians.

Hesychius (5th c. A.D.) Alexandrian lexicographer, author of a comprehensive word list preserved as a "glossary" in a (sole) 15th c. manuscript. Despite the badly preserved state of the MS, the "glossary" remains a valuable source for words whose meanings are otherwise lost or obscured.

Himerius (4th c. A.D.) Greek rhetorician, practicing most of his life in Athens. Author of eighty speeches (forty-two survive) on contemporary subjects. Displays, for the most part, a talent for saying nothing, gracefully and at length.

Julian (the Apostate) (4th c. A.D.) Highly colorful figure. Successful general, statesman, and classical scholar/enthusiast responsible for the reinstitution of pagan cults and the advocacy of classicism, in all its aspects, over Christianity. Proclaimed "Caesar" by the Emperor Constantius II and placed in charge of Gaul and Britain. Later proclaimed "Augustus" by his adoring troops when the Emperor sought to restrict his growing power and popularity.

Longinus (1st c. A.D.) Author of the highly creative and influential *On the Sublime* exploring the qualities of thought and style which mark writing as "sublime." His concern with the moral function of literature and his impatience with pedantry give a clear impression of a serious and original mind.

Lucian (2nd c. A.D.) Rhetorician turned author. Best known for his satiric dialogues and for his still extant *True History* (whose only truth, he tells us at the start, is that all which follows is false).

Maximus of Tyre (2nd c. A.D.) Sophist and itinerant lecturer. Author of forty-one extant *Lectures* which, though showing no philosophic originality, are eloquent exhortations to virtue, decked with quotations, chiefly from Plato and Homer.

Menander (4th and 3rd c. B.C.) Writer of New Comedy. Only one of approximately 100 plays (the *Dyskolos* "Misanthrope") survives intact.

Palatine Anthology The greatest anthology of classical literature consisting of Greek poetic epigrams. So called because the only manuscript was discovered at the Count Palatine's library at Heidelberg (1606). The work is thought to have been compiled by Byzantine scholars, about A.D. 980. It contains some 3,700 epigrams arranged in fifteen books under as many different headings.

Pindar (5th c. B.C.)   Lyric poet whose Epinician, or Victory, Odes survive almost complete. Pindar composed these pieces on commission from victors of the Olympian, Nemean, Pythian and Isthmian Games. The victor's accomplishment, qualities, and pedigree were extolled within the framework of divine myth.

Plutarch (1st and 2nd c. A.D.)   Philosopher and biographer. A most prolific writer, many of whose works survive (though even more are lost). Most influential in Byzantine times and during the Renaissance. His minor works were collected in medieval times under the heading of *Moralia* (*Moral Pieces*), a title now used to cover everything apart from his *Lives* (both of the Caesars -- only *Galba* and *Otho* survive -- and of great men).

scholiast(s)   Author(s) of notes -- or *scholia* preserved in the margins of texts -- which expound or criticize the language or subject matter at hand.

Servius (4th and 5th c. A.D.)   Author of an extensive commentary on the poems of Vergil. The work, designated for school purposes, shows great erudition in its treatment of grammatic, rhetorical, and stylistic points.

Stobaeus (4th and 5th c. A.D.)   Author of an anthology from poets and prose-writers, intended for the instruction of his son, Septimius. Topics range from metaphysics to household economics. The second two of four books deal largely with ethical questions.

Strabo (1st c. B.C. - 1st c. A.D.)   Greek Stoic geographer whose *Geography* is extant in seventeen books. His work is a storehouse of information, an historical geography, and a philosophy of geography.

Syrianus (5th c. A.D.)   Philosopher and rhetorician, author of a commentary on Aristotles' *Metaphysics*.

Synesius (4th and 5th c. A.D.)   Christian Neoplatonist, orator, and poet. Author of some nine hymns, 156 letters, and rhetorical discourses.

VI

SELECTED BIBLIOGRAPHY

(starred items are the most essential
to an introductory appreciation)

Studies

*Bagg, R., "Love, Ceremony and Daydream in Sappho's
Lyrics," *Arion*, Vol. 3 (1964), pp. 44-81.

Boardman, J., and LaRocca, E., *Eros in Greece*, Lon-
don: John Murray Pub. Ltd., 1978.

Bowie, A. M., *The Poetic Dialect of Sappho and Alcae-
us*, New York: Arno, 1981.

*Bowra, C. M., *Greek Lyric Poetry: From Alcman to Si-
monides*, Oxford: Oxford U. Press, 1961, 1967[2].

Calame, C., *Les Choeurs de Jeunes Filles en Grèce
Archaïque*, Vol. I: Morphologie, fonction religi-
euse et sociale; Vol. II: Alcman, Roma: Edizioni
dell'Ateneo & Bizzari, 1977.

Connolly, T. E., *Swinburne's Theory of Poetry*, Al-
bany: State University of New York Press, 1964.

Dover, K. J., "The Poetry of Archilochus," *Fondation
Hardt* (q.v.) pp. 182-212.

----------, *Greek Homosexuality*, Cambridge, Mass.:
Harvard U. Press, 1978.

DuBois, P., "Sappho and Helen," *Arethusa*, Vol. 11
(1978), pp. 88-99.

FONDATION HARDT pour l'étude de l'antiquité clas-
sique, *Entretiens Tome* X: *Archiloque*, Vandoeuvres-
Genève, 1964. Contains seven technical essays and
discussion in English, French and German.

*Fränkel, H., *Early Greek Poetry and Philosophy*, M.
Hadas and J. Willis trans., Oxford: Alden Press,
1963.

Friedrich, P., *The Meaning of Aphrodite*, Chicago: U. of Chicago Press, 1978.

*Grigson, G., *The Goddess of Love: the Birth, Death and Return of Aphrodite*, London: Constable and Company, Ltd., 1976.

*Hallett, J. P., "Sappho and Her Social Context: Sense and Sensuality," *Signs: Journal of Women in Culture and Society*, Vol. 4 (1979), pp. 447-464.

Hooker, J. T., *The Language and Text of Lesbian Poets*, Innsbruck: Inst. f. Sprachwissenschaft d. Univ. Innsbruck, 1977.

Jenkyns, R., *Three Classical Poets: Sappho, Catullus, and Juvenal*, Cambridge, Mass.: Harvard U. Press, 1982.

Kirkwood, G. M., *Early Greek Monody: The History of a Poetic Type*, Ithaca: Cornell U. Press, 1974. Includes essays on Anacreon, Archilochus and Sappho, among others.

Lasserre, F., "Ornements Erotiques dans la Poésie Lyrique Archaïque," in *Serta Turyniana*, J. L. Heller, ed., Urbana: U. of Illinois Press, 1974, pp. 5-33.

*Lefkowitz, M. R., "Critical Stereotypes and the Poetry of Sappho," *Greek, Roman, and Byzantine Studies*, Vol. 14 (1973), pp. 113-123.

----------, "Cultural Conventions and the Persistence of Mistranslation," *The Classical Journal*, Vol. 68 (1972), pp. 21-38.

Marry, J. D., "Sappho and the Heroic Ideal: *erotos arete*," *Arethusa*, Vol. 12 (1979), pp. 71-92.

Nagy, G., "Phaethon, Sappho's Phaon, and the White Rock of Leukas," *Harvard Studies in Classical Philology*, Vol. 77 (1973), pp. 137-177.

*Page, D. L., *Sappho and Alcaeus: an Introduction to the Study of Ancient Lesbian Poetry*, Oxford: Clarendon Press, 1955, 1970[4]. (All Page references, unless otherwise noted, are to this work.)

----------, "Archilochus and the Oral Tradition," *Fondation Hardt* (q.v.), pp. 119-163.

152

*Rankin, H. D., *Archilochus of Paros*, Park Ridge: Noyes Press, 1977.

Raymond, M. B., *Swinburne's Poetics: Theory and Practice*, The Hague: Mouton, 1971. Contains frequent mention of Sappho.

Robinson, D. M., *Sappho and Her Influence*, Boston: Marshall Jones Company, 1924.

Russo, J., "Reading the Greek Lyric Poets (Monodists)," *Arion*, Vol. 1 n.s. (1974), pp. 707-730 (review of Kirkwood, q.v.).

Rutland, W. R., *Swinburne: A Nineteenth Century Hellene* (with some reflections on the Hellenism of modern poets), Oxford: Basil Blackwell, 1931. Engaging personal and scholarly study of Swinburne and his Greek models.

*Segal, C. P., "Eros and Incantation: Sappho and Oral Poetry," *Arethusa*, Vol. 7 (1974), pp. 139-160.

Snell, B., *The Discovery of the Mind*, T. Rosenmeyer trans., New York: Harper and Row, 1966.

Stanford, W. B., *The Sound of Greek: Studies in the Greek Theory and Practice of Euphony*, Berkeley: U. of California Press, 1967.

*Stigers, E. S., "Romantic Sensuality, Poetic Sense: A Response to Hallett on Sappho," *Signs: Journal of Women in Culture and Society*, Vol. 4 (1979), pp. 465-471.

*----------, "Sappho's Private World," *Women's Studies*, Vol. 8 (1981), pp. 47-63.

----------, "Sappho and the Enclosing Goddess," paper delivered at the Fifth Berkshire Conference, Vassar, June, 1981(a).

Symonds, J. A., *Studies of the Greek Poets*, London: Adam and Charles Black, 1902[3].

Turner, E. G., *Greek Papyri: an Introduction*, Princeton: Princeton U. Press, 1968.

*Van Sickle, J., ed., **The New Archilochus**, *Arethusa*, Vol. 9 no. 2, 1976. See § 75, notes.

Weigall, A., *Sappho of Lesbos: Her Life and Times*, New York: Frederick A. Stokes Co., 1932.

*West, M. L., "Burning Sappho," *Maia*, Vol. 22 (1970), pp. 307-330.

Wills, G., "Sappho 31 and Catullus 51," *Greek, Roman, and Byzantine Studies*, Vol. 8 (1967), pp. 167-197.

Critical Editions and Commentaries

Athenaeus, *The Deipnosophists* (*"Doctors at Dinner"*), C. B. Gulick, ed. and trans., New York: G. P. Putnam's Sons, Vols. 1-5; Cambridge, Mass.: Harvard U. Press, Vols. 6-7, 1927-1941.

*Campbell, D. A., *Greek Lyric Poetry: A Selection of Early Greek Lyric, Elegiac and Iambic Poetry*, New York: St. Martin's Press, 1967.

----------, **Greek Lyric I.** *Sappho Alcaeus*, Cambridge, Mass.: Harvard U. Press, 1982. Revised and newly translated edition of Edmonds (q.v.).

D = Diehl, E., *Anthologia Lyrica Graeca*, Lipsiae, 1925, 1942^2, $1949-1952^3$.

Edmonds, J. M., *Lyra Graeca* Vols. I-III, Cambridge, Mass.: Harvard U. Press, 1922-1952.

Evelyn-White, H. G., *Hesiod, the Homeric Hymns and Homerica*, with an English translation, Cambridge, Mass.: Harvard U. Press; London: William Heinemann, 1914.

Farnell, G. S., *Greek Lyric Poetry*, London: Longman's Green, and Co., 1891.

G = Gentili, B., *Anacreon*, Roma: Edizioni dell'-Ateneo, 1958. Introduction, critical text and apparatus, translation (Italian), studies on papyrus fragments.

*Gerber, D. E., *Euterpe: an Anthology of Early Greek Lyric, Elegiac, and Iambic Poetry*, Amsterdam: Hakkert, 1970.

Haines, C. R., *Sappho, the Poems and Fragments*, London: C. Routledge and New York: E.P. Dutton, 1926.

154

LP = Lobel, E. and Page, D. L., *Poetarum Lesbiorum Fragmenta*, Oxford: Clarendon Press, 1955, 1968[3]. Critical texts, apparatus, word indices, manuscript catalogues and testimonia for the complete works of Sappho and Alcaeus.

Page, D. L., *Alcman: The Partheneion*, Oxford: Clarendon Press, 1951.

P = Page, D. L., *Poetae Melici Graeci*, Oxford: Clarendon Press, 1962.

Smyth, H. W., *Greek Melic Poets*, London: Macmillan and Co., 1900.

T = Tarditi, G., *Archilochus*, Roma: Edizioni dell'-Ateneo, 1968. Introduction, testimonia on the poet's life and art, critical text, apparatus, and translation (Italian).

Voigt, E. M., *Sappho et Alcaeus*, Amsterdam: Polak & Van Gennep, 1971. Exhaustive critical edition, supersedes Lobel-Page whose numberings it largely follows.

W = West, M. L., *Delectus ex Iambis et Elegis Graecis*, Oxford: Oxford U. Press, 1980.

Translations (Contemporary)

Ayrton, M., *Archilochos*, London: Secker & Warburg, 1977.

Barnstone, W., *Greek Lyric Poetry*, New York: Schocken, 1962, 1967.

Bernard, M., *Sappho: A New Translation*, Berkeley: U. of California Press, n.d.

Davenport, G., *Archilochos, Sappho, Alkman*, Berkeley: U. of California Press, 1980.

Groden, S. Q., *The Poems of Sappho*, New York: Bobbs-Merrill Co., 1966.

Lattimore, R., *Greek Lyrics*, Chicago: U. of Chicago Press, 1949, 1960[2].

Roche, P., *The Love Songs of Sappho*, New York: Mentor, 1966.

Tarrant, R. J., *Greek and Latin Lyric Poetry in Translation*, Publication of The American Philological Association, 1972. Contains reviews of the above translations with exception of the first.

Translations (Previous)

Cox, E. M., *The Poems of Sappho with Historical & Critical Notes, Translations, and a Bibliography*, London: Williams & Norgate, LTD. New York: Charles Scribner's Sons, 1925. Intended as an update to the H. T. Wharton edition ("comprehensive and satisfactory as far as it went"). Offers new translations "which it is hoped will be acceptable," and papyri finds since 1885. Traces the history of Sappho translations into English from the mid-seventeenth century to Edmonds' *Lyra Graeca*, Vol. 1, 1922. Book concludes with "A Bibliographical List of Printed Books, Chronologically Arranged, Which Refer to Sappho and Her Poems" (from 1470-1922). Most of these are of antiquarian interest. Two merit special citation: *"The Works of Anacreon and Sappho done from the Greek by several hands, etc.* London, 1713. 8 vo. The Sapphic portion is by Ambrose Philips,⁋ and it contains the first translation into English of the Hymn to Aphrodite," and *"The Adventures of Sappho, Poetess of Mytilene. Translation from the Greek Original, newly discovered.* London 1789. 8vo. Apparently the first piece of fiction in English referring to Sappho.† An imaginary composition."

Miller-Robinson, *The Songs of Sappho*, translated into Rimed Verse by Marion Mills Miller, Litt. D., Greek Texts Prepared and Annotated and literally translated in prose by David Moore Robinson, Ph.D., LL.D., New York: Frank-Maurice, Inc. 1925. Elaborate edition, 400 pp., with "Selected Bibliography Supplementary to Wharton's."

⁋See Appendix I, note.

†For the Sapphic tradition in a variety of literatures, see Robinson 1924 and 1925.

*Wharton, H. T., *Sappho: Memoir, Text, Renderings, and a Literal Translation,*[#] London: John Lane and Chicago: A. C. McClurg, 1895[3]; 1885, 1887[2] by David Stott. Pages gold-embossed on top, rough-cut and of slightly disparate sizes to right and bottom. Back of title page contains the motto, *panta kathara tois katharois* ("All things are pure to the pure") and an Emory University seal indicating the Library's March 11, 1965 acquisition of the volume. Title page elaborately signed by original owner Maurice Thompson, himself a translator of Sappho (see "The Sapphic Secret," *Atlantic Monthly*, March 1894).

Bibliographies

Gerber, D. E., "Studies in Greek Lyric Poetry: 1967–1975," *The Classical World*, Vol. 70 (1976-77), pp. 65-157.

_____, "A Survey of Publications on Greek Lyric Poetry Since 1952," *The Classical World*, Vol. 61 (1967-68), pp. 265-279, 317-330, 378-385.

Kirkwood, G. M., "A Survey of Recent Publications Concerning Classical Greek Lyric Poetry," *The Classical World*, Vol. 47 (1953-54) pp. 33-42, 49-54.

[#]See Appendix 1.

158

APPENDIX I

Henry T. Wharton,
Sappho, 1895

(on the earliest editions and
scholarship of Sappho)

PREFACE TO FIRST EDITION

Sappho, the Greek poetess whom more than eighty generations have been obliged to hold without a peer, has never, in the entirety of her works, been brought within the reach of English readers. The key to her wondrous reputation -- which would, perhaps, be still greater if it had ever been challenged -- has hitherto lain hidden in other languages than ours. As a name, as a figure pre-eminent in literary history, she has indeed never been overlooked. But the English-reading world has come to think, and to be content with thinking, that no verse of hers survives save those two hymns which Addison, in the *Spectator*, has made famous -- by his panegyric, not by Ambrose Philips' translation.*

---

*Philips' translation of the *Hymn to Aphrodite* appeared in the *Spectator*, no. 223, 1711, according to Cox (pp. 33-40 *passim*), as part of "the first reasoned criticism of Sappho and her works in English by Joseph Addison." Addison thought Philips' translation the first ever of a Sapphic poem into English. Cox, however, adduces as first the 1652 translation of poet John Hall of Durham "in an uncommon little book, a translation of Longinus on The Sublime" [see $ 2, notes]. Longinus had a second translator in one J. Pultney, 1680, working from a French version of the Greek original. Lack of familiarity with the original -- and the attendant result (see p. 1, n. 1, above) -- seems as old as the oldest translations into English. Notes Cox, "As it is not improbable that Pultney knew no Greek, and as his version is filtered through the French, it is not remarkable

My aim in the present work is to familiarise English readers, whether they understand Greek or not, with every word of Sappho, by translating all the one hundred and seventy fragments that her latest German editor thinks may be ascribed to her:

> Love's priestess, mad with pain and joy of song,
> Song's priestess, mad with joy and pain of love.
> SWINBURNE.

I have contented myself with a literal English prose translation, for Sappho is, perhaps above all other poets, untranslatable. The very difficulties in the way of translating her may be the reason why no Englishman has hitherto undertaken the task. Many of the fragments have been more or less successfully rendered into English verse, and such versions I have quoted whenever they rose above mediocrity, so far as I have been able to discover them.

After an account of Sappho's life as complete as my materials have allowed, I have taken her fragments in order as they stand in Bergk, whose text I have

that in the process the Sapphic meter should have disappeared and that considerable divergence from the original should have developed."

Philips' rendering had few admirers outside of Addison. Robinson (1925, p. 62) refers to the "namby-pamby Ambrose Philips in whose rendering in the *Spectator* (1711) Sappho's 'molten lava is transmogrified into curds and whey' -- as I once heard the late Basil L. Gildersleeve remark" [see postscript]. W. R. Rutland (p. 281) is downright litiginous: "I am not aware that Mr. Ambrose Philips or M. Nicholas Boileau-Despreaux was ever impeached before any jury of moralists for his sufficiently grievous offence. By any jury of poets both would assuredly have been convicted. Now, what they did I have not done. To the best (and bad is the best) of their ability, they have 'done into' bad French and bad English the very words of Sappho."

I have reproduced (from Cox) Philips' and Hall's translations in Appendix IV.

almost invariably followed. I have given (1) the
original fragment in Greek, (2) a literal version in
English prose, distinguished by italic type, (3) every
English metrical translation that seems worthy of such
apposition, and (4) a note of the writer by whom, and
the circumstances under which, each fragment has been
preserved. Too often a fragment is only a single word,
but I have omitted nothing.

It is curious to note how early in the history of
printing the literature of Sappho began. The British
Museum contains a sort of commentary on Sappho which
is dated 1475 in the Catalogue; this is but twenty
years later than the famous 'Mazarin' Bible, and only
one year after the first book was printed in England.
It is written in Latin by Georgius Alexandrinus
Merula, and is of much interest, apart from its
strange type and contractions of words.

The first edition of any part of Sappho was that
of the Hymn to Aphrodite, by H. Stephanus, in his
edition of Anacreon, 8vo, 1554. Subsequent editions of
Anacreon contained other fragments attributed to her,
including some that are now known to be by a later
hand. Fulvius Ursinus wrote some comments on those
then known in the *Carmina Novem Illustrium Feminarum*
published at Antwerp, 8vo, 1568. Is. Vossius gave an
emended text of the two principal odes in his edition
of Catullus, London, 4vo, 1684.

But the first separate edition of Sappho's works
was that of Johann Christian Wolf, which was published
in 4vo at Hamburg in 1733, and reprinted under an
altered title two years later. Wolf's work is as
exhaustive as was possible at his date. He gives a
frontispiece figuring all the then known coins bearing
reference to the poetess; a life of her -- written,

161

like the rest of the treatise, in Latin -- occupies 32 pages; a Latin translation of all the quotations from or references to her in the Greek classics, and all the Latin accounts of her, together with the annotations of most previous writers, and copious notes by himself, in 253 pages; and the work is completed with elaborate indices.

The next important critical edition of Sappho was that of Heinrich Friedrich Magnus Volger, pp. lxviii., 195, 8vo, Leipzig, 1810. It was written on the old lines, and did not do much to advance the knowledge of her fragments. Volger added a 'musical scheme,' which seems more curious than useful, and of which it is hard to understand either the origin or the intention.

But nothing written before 1816 really grasped the Sapphic question. In that year Welcker published his celebrated refutation of the long-current calumnies against Sappho, *Sappho vindicated from a prevailing prejudice*. In his zeal to establish her character, he may have been here and there led into extravagance, but it is certain that his searching criticism first made it possible to appreciate her true position. Nothing that has been written since has succeeded in invalidating his main conclusions, despite all the onslaughts of Colonel Mure and those few who sympathised with him.

Consequently the next self-standing edition of Sappho, by Christian Friedrich Neue, pp. 106, 4vo, Berlin, 1827, embodying the results of the 'new departure,' was far in advance of its predecessors -- not in cumbrous elaboration, but in critical excellence. Neue's life of the poetess was written in the light of Welcker's researches; his purification of the text was due to more accurate study of the ancient manuscripts,

162

assisted by the textual criticisms published by Bishop Blomfield the previous year in the Cambridge *Museum Criticum*.

Since Neue's time much has been written about Sappho, for the most part in Latin or German. The final revisions of the text, and collection of all that can now be possibly ascribed to her, was made by Theodor Bergk, in his *Poetae Lyrici Graeci*, pp. 82-140 of the third volume of the fourth edition, 8vo, Leipzig, 1882, which I have here, with rare exceptions, followed.

There is a noteworthy dissertation on her life by Theodor Kock, *Alkaos und Sappho*, 8vo, Berlin, 1862, in which the arguments and conclusions of Welcker are mainly endorsed, and elaborated with much mythological detail.

Perhaps the fullest account of Sappho which has recently appeared is that by A. Fernandez Merino, a third edition of which was published at Madrid early last year. Written in Spanish, it discusses in an impartial spirit every question concerning Sappho, and is especially valuable for its copious references.

Professor Domenico Comparetti, the celebrated Florentine scholar, to whom I shall have occasion to refer hereafter, has recently done much to familiarise Italian readers with the chief points of Sapphic criticism. His enthusiasm for her character and genius is all that can be desired, but his acceptance of Welcker's arguments is not so complete as mine. Where truth must lie between two extremes, and evidence on either side is so hard to collect and estimate, it is possible for differently constituted minds to reach very different conclusions. The motto at the back of my title-page is the guide I am most willing to

163

follow. But, after all, to use the words of a friend whom I consulted on the subject, 'whether the pure think her emotion pure or impure; whether the impure appreciate it rightly, or misinterpret it; whether, finally, it was platonic or not; seems to me to matter nothing.' Sappho's poetic eminence is independent of such consideration. To her,

> All thoughts, all passions, all delights,
>   Whatever stirs this mortal frame,
> All are but ministers of Love,
>   And feed his sacred flame.

Those who wish to learn more about Sappho than is here recorded will find a guide in the Bibliography which I have added at the end of the volume. My sole desire in these pages is to present 'the great poetess' to English readers in a form from which they can judge of her excellence for themselves, so far as that is possible for those to whom Aeolic Greek is unfamiliar. Her most important fragments have been translated into German, French, Italian, and Spanish, as well as English; but all previous complete editions of her works have been written solely by scholars for scholars. Now that, through the appreciation of Sappho by modern poets and painters, her name is becoming day by day more familiar, it seems time to show her as we know her to have been, to those who have neither leisure nor power to read her in the tongue in which she wrote.

I have not concerned myself much with textual criticism, for I do not arrogate any power of discernment greater than that possessed by a scholar like Bergk. Only those who realise what he has done to determine the text of Sappho can quite appreciate the value of his work. Where he is satisfied, I am content. He wrote for the learned few, and I only strive to popularise the result of such researches as his: to show, indeed, so far as I can, that which centuries of scholarship have succeeded in accomplishing.

The translations by Mr. John Addington Symonds, dated 1883, were all made especially for this work in the early part of that year, and have not been elsewhere published. My thanks are also due to Mr. Symonds for much valuable criticism.

The medallion which forms the frontispiece has been engraved by my friend Mr. John Cother Webb, after the head of Sappho in the picture by Mr. L. Alma Tadema, R.A., exhibited at the Royal Academy in 1881, as 'op. ccxxiii.,' and now in America. I trust that my readers will sympathise with me in cordial gratitude to both artist and engraver, to the one for his permission, to the other for his fidelity.

HENRY T. WHARTON

39 St. George's Road
    Kilburn, London, N.W.,
        May 1885.

APPENDIX II

Sappho*
By Algernon Charles Swinburne

(*The Saturday Review*, Vol. 117, p. 228
21 February 1914)

If there be any truth in the opinion of those judges who hold that the highest and noblest branch of English literature is that of poetry, we may not be far wrong if we proceed from the admission of this flattering truth to the assumption that the fairest and most precious fruit of that branch is to be found in its dramatic outgrowth. The lyric and the dramatic are the two highest forms of the poetic art; it rises and divides itself as it were into these two sovereign peaks or summits at the crowning point of its perfection when it passes out of the narrative or epic stage of its godlike childhood and heroic youth. Above the final result of these forms it never can rise, beyond them it never can pass; and when there is no longer a source in the poetic literature of a nation for fresh development and vigorous increase either on the lyric side or the dramatic, its time is come to pass downward into its period of decadence through the various and often fruitful and beautiful stages of elegiac or idyllic, satiric or didactic verse. But in the poetic literature of a nation really great and rich in that

*Mr. Theodore Watts-Dunton has allowed the *Saturday Review* to print this unpublished appreciation of Sappho, By Algernon Charles Swinburne. Unpublished work, prose or poetry, of Swinburne's is very rare. We are happy, therefore, to print an appreciation so typical, in its glow and passion, of the great poet. It is not a fragment, but is quite complete in itself. It is of singular interest to every reader of Swinburne, because Sappho's fragments exercised an immense influence on his work. We have been told that Swinburne was "steeped in Sappho" [*SR* editor's note].

especial quality of its life, the capacities of such increase and the possibilities of such development are not easily to be limited by definition or prediction. It may be safe to say at certain points of its history that further advance is impossible, if the word advance be taken in the direct and absolute sense of improvement; that a nation which has had its Aeschylus or its Shakespeare has produced men unsurpassable in the dramatic line for ever, as a nation which has brought forth a Sappho or a Shelley has attained a point in lyric poetry beyond which none of its children to come can pass; but it is not even after the birth and death of such as these safe to say of a nation which could bear them that it never can bear their like -- at least, that it never may look to bring forth poets worthy to be names with them.

Judging even from the mutilated fragments fallen within our reach from the broken altar of her sacrifice of song, I for one have always agreed with all Grecian tradition in thinking Sappho to be beyond all question and comparison the very greatest poet that ever lived. Aeschylus is the greatest poet who ever was also a prophet; Shakespeare is the greatest dramatist who ever was also a poet; but Sappho is simply nothing less -- as she is certainly nothing more -- than the greatest poet who ever was at all. Such at least is the simple and sincere profession of my lifelong faith.

APPENDIX III

ALCMAN: Maiden Song
(*Partheneion*)

Translation and introductory note by
Mary R. Lefkowitz*

A chorus of young girls describe themselves
and their ceremonial role in a special song.
They appear to be offering a robe to a god-
dess, possibly Helen, who was worshipped in
Sparta. Their erotic attraction to their
leaders, Hagesichora and her friend Agido,
recalls Sappho's world; perhaps Aenesimbrota
was their teacher and trainer. Emphasis on
the beauty of face and hair suggests that
they are involved in a ritual that marks the
transition (hence perhaps the references to
battle) from girlhood to womanhood: the run-
ning of races is also a feature of puberty
rites for Athena in Argos and Artemis in
Brauron. Comparison to horses may suggest
the imminence of marriage, which is often
described in metaphors of taming and yoking.
Doves frequently represent women's vulnera-
bility. The girls readily accept their
leaders' preeminence. But in men's competi-
tion, success is ordinarily accompanied by
strong expression of envy and resentment.

I sing of Agido's light. I see her as the sun; Agido
calls him to testify to us that he is shining. But our
famous leader will not let me either praise or criti-
cise her; for our leader seems to us to be supreme, as
if one set a horse among the herds, strong, prize-
winning, with thundering hooves -- a horse of the
world of dreams.

*M. R. Lefkowitz and M. B. Fant, *Women's Life in Greece and
Rome*, Baltimore: Johns Hopkins Univ. Press, 1982, p. 119 (by
permission of author).

And don't you see: the race-horse is Venetic; but my
cousin Hagesichora's hair blooms like unmixed gold.
And her silver face -- why should I spell it out? Here
is Hagesichora. And she who is second to Agido in
looks, runs like a Colaxian horse to an Ibenian. For
the Doves bring the robe to the Goddess of the Dawn
for us; they rise like the dog star through the immor-
tal night and fight for us.

There is not enough purple to protect us, nor jewelled
snake of solid gold, nor Lydian cap -- adornment of
girls with their dark eyes; nor Nanno's hair, no nor
Areta who is like the gods; not Sylakis and Cleeisera.
You wouldn't go to Aenesimbrota's house and say: let
me have Astaphis; may Philylla look at me, and lovely
Damareta and Vianthemis -- no, it's Hagesichora who
excites me.

For Hagesichora of the fair ankles is near her; close
to Agido . . . she praises our festival. Yes, gods,
receive [their prayer]. From the gods [comes] accom-
plishment and fulfilment. Leader, I could say -- a
young girl that I am; I shriek in vain from my roof
like an owl, and I will say what will please Dawn
most, for she has been healer of our troubles; but it
is through Hagesichora that girls have reached the
peace they long for . . .

The first published rendering of Sappho
into English
John Hall of Durham 1652
(from E. M. Cox, p. 34)

He that sits next to thee now and hears
Thy charming voyce, to me appears
Beauteous as any Deity
        That rules the skie.

How did his pleasing glances dart
Sweet languors to my ravish'd heart
At the first sight though so prevailed
        That my voyce fail'd.

I'me speechless, feavrish, fires assail
My fainting flesh, my sight doth fail
Whilst to my restless mind my ears
        Still hum new fears.

Cold sweats and tremblings so invade
That like a wither'd flower I fade
So that my life being almost lost,
        I seem a Ghost.

Yet since I'me wretched must I dare.

A Hymn to Venus
Ambrose Philips 1711
(from E. M. Cox, pp. 61-63)

I

O Venus beauty of the skies,
To whom a thousand temples rise,
Gaily false in gentle smiles,
Full of love-perplexing wiles;
O goddess from my heart remove
The wasting cares and pains of love.

II

If ever thou hast kindly heard
A song in soft distress preferred,
Propitious to my tuneful vow,
O gentle goddess hear me now.
Descend thou bright immortal guest
In all thy radiant charms confessed.

III

Thou once didst leave almighty Jove
And all the golden roofs above,
The car thy wanton sparrows drew,
Hovering in air they lightly flew;
As to my bower they winged their way
I saw their quivering pinions play.

IV

The birds dismissed (while you remain)
Bore back their empty car again.
Then you with looks divinely mild
In every heavenly feature smiled,
And asked what new complaints I made
And why I called you to my aid.

V

What frenzy in my bosom raged,
And by what cure to be assuaged,
What gentle youth I would allure
Whom in my artful toils secure,
Who does thy tender heart subdue,
Tell me my Sappho, tell me who.

VI

Though now he shuns thy longing arms,
He soon shall court thy slighted charms,
Though now thy offerings he despise,
He soon to thee shall sacrifice;
Though now he freeze, he soon shall burn
And be thy victim in his turn.

VII

Celestial visitant, once more
Thy needful presence I implore.
In pity come, and ease my grief,
Bring my distempered soul relief,
Favour thy suppliant's hidden fires
And give me all my heart desires.

EDITION CONCORDANCE

Sappho	
Db	LP
1	1
2	31
3	2
4	16
5	95
6	94
7	34
8	96
9	49
10	131
11	57
12	137
13	15b
14	22
15	21b
16	23
17	105a
18	105c
19	114
20	107
21	104a
22	141
23	105D
24	30
25	112
26	44
27	132
28	97
29	110
30	111
31	51
32	50
33	126
34	102
35	47
36	130
37	48
38	(*Fr. Adesp.* 976P)

Alcman	
Db	Dl
39	51
40	3
41	101
42	36
43	94
44	58

Anacreon	
Db	G
45	37
46	25
47	46
48	13
49	78
50	22
51	15
52	83
53	96
54	60
55	19
56	99
57	43
58	28
59	76
60	14
61	5
62	33
63	56
64	38,65
65	111
66	108
67	94
68	84
69	74
70	36

Archilochus	
Db	T
71	203
72	197
73	212
74	111
75	(196aW)
76	109
77	190
78	1
79	2
80	96
81	105
82	8
83	102
84	16
85	44
86	43
87	118
88	112
89	25,26
90	27

Ibycus	
Db	Dl
91	6
94	7

An Alma Mater Postscript

I am prompted by mention of Basil Gildersleeve
(p. 160), though I run the risk of sentiment, to con-
clude on a personal, if not discursive, note. Gilder-
sleeve was the first faculty appointment (1876) and
University Professor of Greek at The Johns Hopkins
University. He was founding editor of the *American
Journal of Philology* (1880), the oldest Classics
journal in North America. David Robinson, prominent
lyric authority of his time, was "Vickers Professor of
Archeology and Epigraphy, and Lecturer on Greek Liter-
ature in the Johns Hopkins University." I recall with
much fondness my first reading of Greek lyric at Johns
Hopkins under the inspired direction of Professor
Gregory Nagy whose own comparative studies in Epic and
Lyric have received broad acclaim. My two closest col-
leagues in Atlanta, Janice and Herbert Benario, both
received their Ph.D's in Classics at Johns Hopkins. At
the 1982 meeting of the Classical Association of the
Middle West and South, Southern Section, Herbert
Benario presided over a panel commemorating the
Gildersleeve legacy. I acquired the Cox (1925) trans-
lation of Sappho, from which I have taken much plea-
sure and instruction, from bookdealer Carl Berkowitz,
Chester, New York, himself a Hopkins M.A. in Classics.
The volume was inscribed on Christmas Day 1928 with a
two-stanza Ode to Eleanor and was given her as a gift.
Unknown to Berkowitz until he described the volume by
phone, the pages concealed the accompanying newspaper
clipping (1933) -- an unlikely item, perhaps, but one
which yet calls to be rescued from oblivion.

FLIER WHO SOARS IN STUDIES

MISS ELEANOR LAY

Proving herself not only a capable aviatrix, but a high flier in the scholastic realm, Miss Eleanor Lay, graduate student at Syracuse University, was named Wednesday as recipient of a graduate scholarship at John Hopkins University, where she will specialize in Latin, archeology and Greek as a candidate for a degree of doctor of philosophy. She is also Syracuse's best known woman pilot.